How to Encourage Others

How to Encourage Others

Bill G. Bruster and Robert D. Dale

BROADMAN PRESS
Nashville, Tennessee

Unless marked otherwise, Scriptures are quoted from the King James Version.
Verses marked TLB are taken from *The Living Bible.* Copyright © Tyndale House
Publishers, Wheaton, Illinois, 1971. Used by permission.

Verses marked RSV are from the Revised Standard Version of the Bible,
copyrighted 1946, 1952, © 1971, 1973.

BV
4211.2
.B72

Dewey Decimal Classification: 251
Subject Heading: PREACHING // MINISTRY
Library of Congress Catalog Card Number: 82-70868
Printed in the United States of America

Foreword

"If I had my life to live over," a famous pastor lamented, "I would preach more encouragement to my congregation." Encouragement. We all need encouragement, and we need it all the time.

Encouragement wears many faces. One of encouragement's most familiar faces is proclaiming the gospel—preaching, teaching, and evangelizing. Another well-known face of encouragement is caring—support in grief, daily pressures, family needs, and vocational concerns. This book illustrates the strong link between biblical preaching and Christian care. Quality ministry—both lay and professional—shares Christ's grace in both word and deed.

Each chapter of this book contains a what-to-do segment reflecting ministry insights and a what-to-say sermon summary. This book reflects a team effort. Bob Dale provided the Christian care materials and Bill Bruster the biblical sermons. The different materials are set in contrasting type. Together we hope they provide you both information and inspiration for a ministry of encouragement.

Contents

1

Christians Need Encouragement, Too!

Encouragement is an important Christian ministry. Only in fiction does right always win, truth always triumph, and people always live happily ever after. In real life there are Judases to betray us and crosses to crush us as well as victories to enjoy and share. We live in a mixed world—good and bad, right and wrong. Wheat and tares grow together, and rain falls on the just and unjust person. All of us—Christians too—need encouragement to live happily and well.

More Than Conquerors

Kipling described the key to happy living as meeting triumph and disaster, "both of these imposters," just the same. He saw a pivotal truth—the values we live by are more important than the circumstances we live in. Throughout history persons have achieved and contributed in spite of adversity. Milton was blind but wrote beautiful poetry. Beethoven was deaf but composed unforgettable music. Helen Keller was deaf, dumb, and blind but overcame her handicaps and inspired millions of persons. Pasteur was partially paralyzed but became father of modern bacteriology. Julius Caesar was epileptic but rose to fame and infamy. Winston Churchill was born with a speech impediment but developed into an international leader. Lincoln, Shakespeare, Handel, Dickens, and George Washington Carver were born in poverty but overcame their beginnings to enrich our world. As Harry Emerson Fosdick said, "The great work of the world has been done by handicapped persons."

Paul, who personally experienced the highs and lows of normal living, testified, "In all these things we are more than conquerors through him who loved us" (Rom. 8:37). Christ helps us bear our burdens and celebrate our joys.

Joe Ingram tells a lovely story of Christ's encouragement of his children. A man dreamed he walked along a beach with Jesus. The sky served as a giant screen upon which scenes from his life were projected. Most of the scenes depicted two sets of footprints—his and those of Jesus.

Suddenly he noticed some scenes—the lowest and saddest times of his life—had only one set of footprints. The man began to question and accuse Jesus. "Lord," he complained, "when I decided to follow you, you promised to be with me always. Yet, when my life was at its low ebbs, there was only one set of footprints. Why did you desert me when I needed you most?"

In the man's dream, Jesus answered, "I never left you when life became difficult. At the places where you saw only one set of footprints, I was carrying you." Christ encourages us.

Christians aren't immune from the demands, pressures, and crises of life. When I inventory the lives of Christian acquaintances during the past year, I recall these opportunities for encouragement:

- A wife and mother coping with terminal cancer;
- A family with a child facing prison on drug charges;
- The divorce of a promising young couple;
- The death of a husband and father in a motor accident;
- A family in which all the children were suffering from broken legs at the same time;
- A young, single woman facing a hysterectomy;
- The murder of an innocent bystander during a convenience store robbery;

- The drowning of a young mother and child;
- Five firemen killed in an explosion during an industrial fire;
- A church sanctuary destroyed by fire.

We Christians face all the garden-variety accidents, diseases, and disappointments of the human race. Life isn't as the Madison Avenue advertisers or the religious success vendors present it. Christians need encouragement, and we get encouragement from each other and from the Spirit of Christ, the Great Encourager (John 14:16-17).

Encouragement in Action

But what does an encourager do? Barnabas is a Bible hero where encouragement is concerned. His nickname was "Son of encouragement" (Acts 4:36, RSV). While his story is briefly told in the New Testament, Barnabas's ministry included at least five major acts of encouragement.

First, Barnabas encouraged persons to make a fresh start in life. Paul's first encounter with the Jerusalem church shows Barnabas's gift of encouragement (Acts 9:26-30). The Jerusalem Christians excluded Paul. They likely wondered if his Damascus Road conversion were genuine and feared he might be a spy to infiltrate church ranks, but Barnabas acted as Paul's sponsor. Paul made a fresh start as a Christian minister and missionary because Barnabas vouched for him. An encourager knows Christ makes new persons who deserve a fresh start in life.

Second, Barnabas encouraged persons to bridge the old and the new. Barnabas was born a Jew in the Greek world (Acts 4:36); he understood the religious perspective of both worlds. When the early church launched its bold mission thrust into the Gentile world, it was Barnabas who led the ministry in Antioch (Acts 11:22) and on the first missionary journey (Acts 13:1-3). Change is always an occasion for encouragement. When the old and the new collide, encouragers are needed.

Third, Barnabas encouraged persons when they faced economic uncertainty. The first time Barnabas appears in the saga of salvation he is noted as an example of Christian generosity (Acts 4:32-37). Later, the Antioch Christians gathered an offering for their famine-stricken brothers and sisters in Jerusalem. Barnabas was dispatched as a trustworthy friend to deliver the gift (Acts 11:27-30). When persons are pressed financially and fear they won't be able to provide for themselves and their families, encouragement is timely.

Fourth, Barnabas encouraged persons to accept a second chance. John Mark, a relative of Barnabas, joined Paul and Barnabas on the first missionary journey, but John Mark turned back in midtrip (Acts 13:13). When the second missionary tour was being planned, Barnabas wanted to include John Mark on the team again. Paul vigorously refused. Paul and Barnabas then split up and formed two missionary teams. Barnabas believed in John Mark when he was trying to overcome a quitter's reputation, and John Mark, probably the author of the earliest Gospel, grew into a mature Christian. Encouragement is a key ingredient in supporting persons who are ready to risk a second chance.

Fifth, Barnabas encouraged persons to grow as Christians. When Barnabas went to Antioch, he saw his role as strengthening the young Christians there (Acts 11:23-24). After he had exhausted his own teaching resources, he brought Paul to Antioch and together their encouragement helped the believers deserve a unique name—"Christians." Christian growth rarely happens in isolation. An encouraging word from another Christian person or group guides and strengthens us for the next step in the pilgrimage of faith.

Profile of an Encourager

Barnabas is a model for the ministry of encouragement. Like any Christian encourager Barnabas had several basic qualities. A catalog of supportive attributes follows:

• Willingness to risk. An encourager has to stick his neck out, but risk can pay dividends. An Arab proverb reminds us, "You may forget with whom you laughed, but you will never forget with whom you wept." It takes courage to encourage others.

• Unselfishness and hard work. I once met a young man who was really "under the circumstances." He was in trouble at home, on the job, and with the law. As a result, he became suicidal. Over the Thanksgiving holidays he called me at home fifteen or twenty times. We had family guests, and after several calls my patience began to wear thin. I had listened and encouraged him up to my limits, but I decided to hang in there with him just a bit longer. As his pain subsided, he told me something that made all the hours of work worthwhile. "You've shown more care to me these past few days," he said, "than anyone has before in my whole life." The supreme effort of encouraging others often pays off.

• Ability to see Christ in others. One of the most haunting of Jesus' stories is the sheep and goat judgment (Matt. 25:31-46). The judgment of the persons involved was based on how they had responded to others' needs—the hungry, sick, and imprisoned. Interestingly, none had seen Christ in human hurts (Matt. 25:37-39,44). The encourager senses the "incognito Christ" who is masked behind the pain of persons. When we encourage others, we serve Christ.

• Capacity to do the simple things. In the account mentioned above, simple acts of ministry are crucial. Food, drink, or a visit count as crucial ministry actions. No one needs a million dollars or great beauty or enormous knowledge to be an encourager. A cup of cold water can be a lifesaver. Recently I heard a man almost explode with frustration. "No one," he complained, "ever asked me what kind of day I'd had!" To thoughtfully inquire how another's life is going is a small act within the reach of any Christian. Encouragement can be practiced by all.

• Faith in the future. Life yields some severe blows, but the encourager believes there's hope in God, that the Lord will make tomorrow better for us. Yesterday may be full of lessons, but tomorrow is brimful of new possibilities in the purpose of God. The encourager lives out of this faith and hope.

• Wholesomeness. The encourager is a good person. That's one of the qualities of Barnabas (Acts 11:24). Wholesomeness is a basic ingredient of encouragement.

Encouragement's Cycle

In the Badlands of South Dakota my car overheated one hot August day. I asked a dozen fellow travelers for water and only got frightened looks signaling, *If I give you water, I may need it next myself.* Finally, a huge man offered me the water from an ice chest, and it filled my car's radiator. When I tried to pay him for the water, he declined with a smile and replied, "If you're ever in Fayetteville, Arkansas, stop and see me!"

Two days later a few miles south of Wounded Knee, South Dakota, I saw a slender man standing beside a car with a plume of steam rising into the air. I stopped and helped the stranded family find and install a new top radiator hose. As I prepared to leave, the car's owner offered to pay me for my help. When I declined, he smiled and said, "If you're ever in Fayetteville, Arkansas, stop and see me!"

For an electric instant I thought I'd heard an echo, but I'd only heard the natural cycle of encouragement. I had received help, and I had given help.

Encouragement runs in a cycle. When we become a Barnabas to others, a Christian encourager, we never give out. Rather we fill up. Encouragers are a blessing—and they are blessed.

Encouraging is helping. And giving support. And providing hope. And lending confidence. And Christians need encouragement, too.

I

ENCOURAGEMENT FOR LIFE'S PRESSURES

2
Healing "Hurry Up" Sickness

Stress bothers all of us occasionally. Only the degree of our stress differs from person to person and time to time. Take the case of Ara Parseghian, for instance. For eleven years Parseghian was successful as head football coach at Notre Dame University, but winning 82 percent of Notre Dame's tough football games took its toll on Parseghian. The fifty-two-year-old coach quit college football at the end of the 1974 season. The reason? Stress.

Nineteen seventy-four was a stress-filled year for Parseghian. Three close friends died. One daughter married; the other daughter suffers from multiple sclerosis. Six players were kicked off his team by university disciplinary actions. Injuries caused the loss of other key players. His national championship team from 1973 ranked ninth in the 1974 polls at the end of the season when Parseghian stepped down.

Listen to his candid description of his personal stress:

> I just need time to rejuvenate myself. I am physically and emotionally drained. This is not an impulsive decision. I've been mulling over this in my head for some time now, and I finally decided at midseason that my health and the welfare of my family was more important than anything else.

Stress wears us down.

Stress—Good or Bad?

Stress is life's wear and tear on the body, according to Hans Selye, an expert on stress and its effects. Others simply call stress the "hurry up" sickness. Most of us know stress as a feeling of pressure, a sense of being a bit out of balance. Stress occurs when we experience a threat and try to adapt to the alarm signals. Because of modern society's pressures, some medical researchers call stress the fastest-growing disease in the western world and claim 70 percent of illness is stress induced.

Not all stress is destructive. While stress is usually thought of as painful "distress," some stress is pleasant "eustress." Moderate stress is actually the spice of life and gives us stimulation and challenge. In fact, the absolute absence of stress is death. So some stress is good for us, but constant stress erodes our mental and physical reserves.

Several years ago I felt stress keenly, stopped, evaluated my life, and wrote this "declaration of dependence."

- I need a daily time of meditation and spiritual refreshment.
- I need regular, strenuous exercise.
- I need both a backlog and a bombardment of quality strokes.
- I need caring friends and listeners.
- I need to practice the managerial skills of delegation and time use more effectively.
- I need a day off each week and a vacation period each month.
- I need to say no to extra outside opportunities and demands.
- I need to learn to accept help rather than only playing the helper.
- I need the love and support of my mate and children.
- I need to worship instead of always leading worship.
- I need to refocus my dream and reclarify my values.
- I need to reestablish my personal and emotional stability zones.
- I need to balance my workaholism off against playful re-creation.

- I need to stop and smell the roses.
- I need to learn the difference between being a messiah and a steward.
- I need to write more and speak to scattered groups less.
- I need to trim off a few pounds and eat more wisely.

These renewed priorities helped me feel a greater sense of control over my life.

What Turns the Pressure Up?

What causes stress? Anything that turns the pressure up on you. Anything that knots your stomach, tightens your neck and shoulder muscles, or makes your head throb.

For some people stress is related to the kind of work they do. We imagine that policemen, air traffic controllers, and surgeons have high-pressure jobs, but other occupations are actually even more stressful. According to the National Institute for Occupational Safety and Health, jobs causing most emotional distress are those working *with the public* in settings over which the workers have *little control*. The most stressful jobs are those of health technicians, waiters, practical nurses, inspectors, musicians, public relations people, lab technicians, dishwashers, warehousemen, and nurse's aides. They do "people work" but feel they have minimal control over their work situations.

Your personal life-style can cause stress too. Stress attacks the weakest biological and chemical links in our bodies and triggers heart attacks, ulcers, high blood pressure, diarrhea, and headaches. Medical researchers Friedman and Rosenman found we have either Type A or Type B personalities. The Type A person is aggressive, competitive, impatient, and always in a hurry. Unsure of his worth, he works out his salvation by making more money and accumulating more symbols of success. He's a prime candidate for heart attack and artery disease. Type B personalities are as ambitious as Type A personalities but live more relaxed and longer. The Type B person is also more apt to be a churchgoer and give faith precedence over money, numbers, and power.

Overwork also adds to stress. Self-management is a practical challenge for all of us—especially those of us who are workaholics, addicted to our jobs as surely as a drunk is to his bottle. Some of us feel guilty if we're not working. "The bow too tensely strung is easily broken" notes the proverb. When work stretches us to the breaking point, stress is usually present.

Change can put us under stress too. Seattle psychiatrists Holmes and Rahe discovered change has a snowballing effect—too much change in too short a time makes us physically and emotionally sick. Some changes are obviously more traumatic than others; your spouse's death or a divorce create more turmoil than a traffic ticket or going on vacation.

Holmes and Rahe ranked the forty-three most stressful life changes and assigned a numerical value to each change. They also predicted the chances of illness a person runs who has accumulated certain point totals of change within one year. For example, if a minister moves to a new church, his change total will reach roughly 300 points, or an 80 percent chance of getting sick in the near future. Change is stressful.

Saying No to Distress

Stress can be moderated and coped with. While no approach is foolproof, several strategies will help you keep stress from turning into distress.

● Anticipate change and plan in advance. Surprises put us under pressure; planning for changes lets us make decisions and adjustments more slowly.

• Evaluate your priorities. We can live a day only once. That means we need to learn to do first things first. Set realistic goals, expect some successes and some failures, and check your progress regularly to make sure your goals are still worthwhile to you. When you must adjust your priorities, change what you can and accept what you can't change.

• Guard your health. Good health is stress insurance. The healthier you are, the more easily you can cope with stress. Plenty of exercise and rest, a balanced diet, and cultivating other interests—family, relaxation and recreation, hobbies, opportunities to serve others—help you resist stress. In crisis situations, like the death of a loved one or a major change, take special steps to be good to yourself.

• Learn to blow off steam. Feelings need to be vented. Otherwise, our pent-up emotions turn inward and eat on us. A supportive relationship is an absolute necessity when stress confronts us. Talk out your problems with a friend or counselor.

• Pace yourself. Running in high gear all of the time is a sure way to burn yourself out. Learn to do one thing at a time. Some businesses now create a "quiet hour" for their executives so key people can recuperate and concentrate on major tasks for sixty uninterrupted minutes. A daily devotional time is an excellent spiritual refreshment opportunity.

• Faith offsets stress. Our faith in Christ is our ultimate weapon against stress. Imagine these stresses on one woman: widowed; a son killed in war; two sons the victims of political assassins; a mentally retarded daughter; a daughter killed in a plane crash. All of these stresses have happened to Rose Kennedy, the mother of President John F. Kennedy. Yet she remains a hopeful person. How? Religious faith.

Mrs. Kennedy has found faith conquers stress. She states,

> I have come to the conclusion that the most important
> element in human life is faith. From faith, and through it, we
> come to a new understanding of ourselves and all the world
> about us. It puts everything into a spiritual focus . . . so that
> love, and joy, and happiness, along with worry, sorrow, and
> loss, become a part of a large picture which extends far
> beyond time and space.

Christ conquers our stresses.

Coping with Stress

Sermon Text: Luke 8:41-56

In October of 1978, I watched the president of the United
States deliver his message on inflation. I had not seen the
president on live television for a number of months and was
amazed at what I saw. The lines and wrinkles in his face had
grown remarkably deep. A man cannot possibly live under the
tensions the president experiences everyday without aging
considerably. Stress has a way of doing that to you.

Jesus was under a lot of stress at this period in his life. This
story in Luke 8 begins with Jesus and his disciples crossing
the Sea of Galilee to seek some rest among the Gadarenes. Like
any of us, even the Son of God had his limits. He was sensitive
enough to recognize his limits and to do something about
them. However, as soon as he and his disciples landed, their
desire for peace was shattered by the frightening spectacle of a
deranged man running loose among the tombstones. Jesus
took time from his rest to deal with this pathetic schizo-
phrenic. When the townspeople arrived, they found the man
clothed and sane. Having accomplished his healing task, Jesus
started back to the side of Galilee's sea he had come from. A

great multitude of people lined the shore to hear him teach. Just as he had begun his message, Jairus, a well-known Jewish leader, rushed forward, exclaiming that his little daughter was at the point of death. He requested Jesus to come immediately and lay his hands upon her. Just as Jesus started for the home of Jairus, the people began to press around him. Out of that multitude came the touch of a woman who had been sick for twelve years. She had spent all of her money trying to find a cure. She touched Jesus expecting to be healed.

Notice the pressure Jesus was under. He had not found the rest he had desired. The people wanted to hear him teach. He was trying to go on a mission of mercy for a man with a dying daughter. A woman out of the crowd clamored for his attention before he left. He could well have been thinking, *Am I going to get to the home of Jairus in time? Will I be able to do anything for this child?* On the other hand, he must have been thinking about the rest that he needed. He must have been thinking about the woman who was desperately reaching out to him for help. The stress on him must have been almost unbearable.

Another character here is caught in stress—Jairus. Luke 8:42 tells us this sick, twelve-year-old child was his only daughter. She had so much of her life ahead of her. Now it was about to ebb away. Jairus was a father torn by the heartbreak of seeing his only daughter die and finding her only source of help coming from a man his employers despised. Jairus was living with tension.

Parents discover stress is a part of raising children. Our feelings run the gamut from concern about their helplessness as infants to outright worry over their recklessness as young adults. Many of us feel the tension between taking care of our own aging parents and our responsibilities with our immediate family. How many of you are feeling the stress of trying to satisfy an employer who expects more from you than you think you are able to give? How many of you are feeling the stress of failing health? Stress is a very real problem in today's world.

First, when we seek help from available sources, we can

cope with stress. "And, behold, there cometh one of the rulers of the synagogue, Jairus by name; and when he saw him, he fell at his feet, And besought him greatly, saying, My little daughter lieth at the point of death: I pray thee, come and lay thy hands on her, that she may be healed; and she shall live" (Mark 5:22-23). Jairus was a man of considerable importance. Barclay notes:

> The Ruler of the Synagogue was the administrative head of the Synagogue. He was the president of the board of elders who were responsible for the good management of the Synagogue. He was responsible for the conduct of the services. He did not usually take part in them himself, but he was responsible for the allocation of duties, and for seeing that they were carried out with all seemliness and good order. The Ruler of the Synagogue was one of the most important and the most respected men in the community.[1]

What would the Jewish religious leaders think if Jairus went to this young upstart Galilean for help? Jesus was clearly in conflict with organized Jewish religion. When Jairus went to Jesus for help, it was like a Chevrolet car salesman driving a Ford for his personal use. It was like a United Airlines pilot flying Delta when he went on vacation. Such things are not done. But Jairus was living with the tension of a dying daughter. Under such tension, we seek help from any source.

Doug Ezell, a Texas seminary professor, was on his way to preach in a small town near Fort Worth one rainy, winter, Sunday morning. He pulled up to a stop sign in a little town eight or ten miles from his destination. His car stalled and wouldn't start again. He got out of his car, raised the hood, and couldn't see anything at all wrong with his automobile. He then began trying to stop people on their way to church. Twenty-five or thirty cars passed him by. They pulled up to the stop sign, took a look at his stalled car, and continued on rather than be late for Bible teaching. Then an old Texas ranch hand pulled up in his pickup truck. Doug looked at the tobacco juice squirted along the driver's door, the gun racks in the back window, the big chew in the guy's jaw, and decided that it would be worthless to stop an ornery cuss like that for help.

Almost on impulse he halfway tried to slow him down. Doug was desperate. A group of folks were meeting for church soon and expected him to preach. He wasn't going to make it. Then the fellow in the pickup pulled over. He tried to help Doug start his car, with no success. He asked Doug where he was going. Doug told him. The fellow told Doug he could drop him off at his house, and Doug could take his pickup to church. It isn't always the people you expect to help you who do.

We often encounter help in unexpected ways. We often encounter God in the most unexpected places and the most unexpected people. When you feel under stress, don't eliminate any possible source of help. Be open to help from anywhere. Don't let your racial prejudices keep you from accepting help from someone of a different race. Don't let your class prejudices keep you from accepting help from people who are rich or poor. Don't let your religious prejudices keep you from receiving help from a Jewish or Catholic friend. Don't let your male-female prejudices keep you from accepting help from a person of the opposite sex. When you are under stress be open to help from any source.

Second, do your best and then be patient when stress drives help away. The Bible says, "And Jesus went with him; and much people followed him, and they thronged him. And a certain woman, which had an issue of blood twelve years" (Mark 5:24-27) began to follow Jesus. This woman saw in his kind look and his compassionate touch her only source of hope. She, too, was living under stress and wanted help from Jesus. So amid the crowd of people surrounding him, she reached out and touched him. He could easily have said, "Why bother me? I'm a busy man. Can't you see the crowd waiting? Didn't you hear the request of Jairus? I have more than a day's work for me here. Couldn't you come back some other day?" But that's not the way Jesus reacted. He stopped and asked, "Who touched me?"

Imagine what was going on in Jairus's mind. He must have been almost frantic. He must have been thinking, *Why is Jesus stopping? Doesn't he know how sick my daughter is? Didn't I tell him she was about to die? Doesn't he care that my daughter could be dead if we don't go right on? What did Jesus mean, "Who touched me"? Hundreds of people are touching him. Is he going to wait and talk to everyone who has touched him? Oh, so it is that sick woman who touched him. I've known her for years. She was sick when my daughter was born. She used to be a wealthy woman, but she spent everything she had trying to be cured. She's been sick at least twelve years. She will live until tomorrow, but if Jesus doesn't hurry my daughter will not live another day. It is now or never as far as my daughter is concerned.*

Then, perhaps, Jairus's mood changed: *Jairus, get hold of yourself. Look how you are reacting. You came to ask this man for help. You've laid your request clearly before him. What else can you do? He's under no obligation to you. He said he would come. I've done my best. I've had every doctor available to see my daughter. Now Jesus will come. If there is help available, he will give it. I must be patient.*

A woman once told Billy Sunday she had a bad temper; but, she observed, her tantrums were over in a minute. He replied, "So is a shotgun blast, but it blows everything to pieces." Impatience usually blows everything to pieces. When we are under stress, our tendency is often to become impatient and go to pieces. The opposite reaction—doing our best and remaining calm—is better.

Third, surround yourself with people of faith when you're coping with stress. "While he yet spake, there came from the ruler of the synagogue's house certain which said, Thy daughter is dead: why troublest thou the Master any further? As soon as Jesus heard the word that was spoken, he saith unto the ruler of the synagogue, Be not afraid, only believe. And he suffered no man to follow him, save Peter, and James, and John the brother of James" (Mark 5:35-37). When Jairus got back home with Jesus and his disciples, he was met by a group of people who informed him his daughter had already died. These messengers seemed to delight in telling bad news. As the crowd looked on in sympathetic silence, all hope must have faded from that father's face. Tears must have welled up in his eyes. His hurt was obvious. But Jesus said, "Be not afraid, only believe."

Then Jesus did a strange thing. He took Peter, James, John, Jairus, and the girl's mother with him into the room where the girl had died. Why did Jesus take Peter, James, and John with him? The people began to laugh at Jesus and make fun of him for going into the house where the dead girl was lying (Mark 5:40). They were people without faith, doubters. Jesus only took those who believed with him. Jesus prayed, and the girl began to show signs of life. Her eyelids began to flutter. Her cheeks began to turn pink. A smile began to play back and forth upon her lips. Her parents caressed her in their arms. Joy was restored to that home. Stress and tension found relief. A family had learned what belief was all about when they were surrounded by people of faith.

In our periods of pressure we may be tempted to abandon faith. If we are to ever live through tension, we must have faith. What if the Wright brothers had listened to the skeptics? We might not be flying today. Where would we be in medical research today had our doctors heeded the skeptics? What if our scientists had heeded those who said we would never go to the moon? Slavery would still be practiced in America today if our forefathers had heeded skeptics. Our main mode of transportation would still be the horse and buggy if our ancestors had listened to the skeptics. Progress is never made without faith. Anytime you are under tension and pressure, surround yourself with the people of faith.

As a boy I was quite poor. My dad was a sharecropper in

southwest Oklahoma. We only lived a half mile or so from
Fincher's Grocery Store. One of the real treats of my boyhood
was to go to Fincher's store and get a cold bottle of pop when
Dad was there on business. I remember a tense situation when
Dad gave me permission to get a bottle of pop. It was not an
everyday treat. For a long time I studied the various kinds of
pop and finally made my decision. I took the bottle and
removed the cap. As I did, the soda pop began to spew
everywhere. In a fraction of a moment, I despaired. Here on a
special occasion a precious bottle of pop was being wasted. I
didn't know what to do. My dad barked out at me, "Don't just
stand there, Billy. Put your mouth over it. Drink it." It was
some of the best advice he ever gave me. I saved most of my
soda pop, because I did something. Had I just stood there and
watched it all spew out, my tension would have been almost
unbearable. I'm sure tears would have been mixed with the
pop on the floor. But I didn't just stand there. I did something. I
put my mouth over it, and I drank it.

When you are faced with stress—move off high center, take
action, do something positive.

Note

1. William Barclay, *The Gospel of Mark* (Philadephia: The Westminster
Press, 1956), p. 126.

3

Blues, Stay Away from My Door!

Ever have one of those days when everything goes wrong? Maybe you felt *Murphy's* Law had become the blueprint of your life:

Nothing is as easy as it looks.
Everything takes longer than you think.
Left to themselves, things always go from bad to worse.
Nothing is lost until you begin to look for it.
If anything can go wrong, it will.

A "down day" is aggravation!

Has a down day stretched into a bad week or month? Did you feel blue, glum, and overwhelmed by your situation in life? Did you feel life was hopeless and want to give up? That's depression! You can do something constructive when the blues won't stay away from your door.

Indicators of Depression

Listen to the following statements for some key indicators of depression:

• "I feel tired all the time." Fatigue and listlessness may be your body's signal you're emotionally down.

• "I don't enjoy life anymore." When you feel sad, apathetic, and disinterested in the things you formerly enjoyed, depression may have set in. As my son once said, "I'm not having fun—any!" No fun for an extended period of time may indicate you're depressed.

● "I'm not sleeping very well." Sleep disturbances—like lying awake for extended periods in the middle of the night—are often a clue to depression.

● "I feel like I'm moving in slow motion on the inside." Depressed persons sometimes can't concentrate and lack the energy to see work through to completion.

● "I'm not worth much any more." Worry and self-questioning are common signs of depression. When you're depressed, all of the "shoulds" of your life march by in an unending line. The result is an inner conversation: *I should do this. I should do that. I can't seem to get anything done. I'm worthless. Why can't I do anything I should do anymore?*

● "I hurt all over inside." Depression is painful. Your very soul aches. Emotional pain is real.

● "I've been down a long time." Prolonged duration is an important indicator of real depression. Duration separates depression from a "down day."

One or two of the indicators listed above may not be caused by depression. But if most or all of these clues show up in a cluster, you're probably depressed and need to talk to someone about it promptly.

What Causes Depression?

A variety of changes, losses, or upsets can trigger occasions of depression. If you're feeling blue and depressed, ask yourself two questions; you may discover some reasons for being "under the circumstances," as a friend of mine describes depression.

First, ask, "Am I angry at someone or something?" When you can't or don't ventilate your anger, it often turns in on you. In fact, depression is often referred to as self-aggression. Depression is an "instead of" ailment. Instead of letting your angry feelings go, you may trap them inside you. Talking and exercising release pent-up anger and keep you from getting depressed.

Second, ask, "Who really cares about me?" When you're cut off from persons who really value you, you can begin to doubt your worth. Without "strokes," you are unsure you're cared for. Institutions too big to fight or problems too complicated to solve easily—like inflation—can leave us feeling isolated and defeated. Surround yourself with people you care about and who care for you. It's a great way to defend yourself against become depressed.

Depression and the Religious Person

Depression isn't a new problem, of course. It popped up in the lives of characters throughout the Bible. Moses felt crushed by an overly heavy sense of responsibility (Num. 11:14 ff). Elijah felt isolated and then won a victory. While he was feeling the natural letdown following any peak experience, he added to his down feelings by exhausting himself physically (1 Kings 18—19). Jonah became angry with God and felt life wasn't worth continuing (Jonah 4).

Depression is a special problem for the religious person. We are conscientious. We strive for perfection. We feel guilt keenly when we fail or think we've failed. We accept heavy responsibility. We expect to live on the mountaintop all of the time. We don't express our anger with God very well. Like Moses, Elijah, and Jonah, we give depression an open door by our life-style.

Yet the Christian knows pardon. We have tasted the heady flavors of a fresh start. We know God has forgiven us and continues to forgive us daily as we confess our sins. That's a basic remedy for depression.

What Can You Do About Depression?

Several actions can help you deal constructively with depression. Try these steps to uncover the silver lining inside your temporarily dark clouds of life:

● Remember it's natural to feel a letdown after a major victory in life or when confronted with a major change, problem, or loss. It's OK to feel depressed occasionally. We all know how the blues feel.

● Women and elderly persons are slightly more apt to become depressed. They more often have a sense of being left out and overlooked in our kind of world. The middle-aged man also is a likely candidate for the blues. Holidays and other occasions for joy and family gatherings remind a depressed person his life is out-of-joint.

● Time often cures depression. The blues usually run in a cycle—down, then up again. A few down days are probably perfectly normal if you can see an obvious situation—like an argument or a death—that could take the wind out of your sails. Hang in there, and you'll probably find yourself on the upswing soon.

James J. Corbett, former heavyweight boxing champion, gave some good advice about struggling against defeat:

> Fight one more round. When your feet are so tired that you have to shuffle back to the center of the ring, fight one more round. When your arms are so tired that you can hardly lift your hands to come on guard, fight one more round. When your nose is bleeding and your eyes are black and you are so tired that you wish your opponent would crack you one on the jaw and put you to sleep, fight one more round—remembering that the man who always fights one more round is never whipped.

Take the attitude of "this too will pass," and it likely will. Patience and persistence pay off.

● Exercise often helps overcome depression. Depression makes your body and mind want to shut down. Some counselors now urge their depressed clients to walk or jog to help them break through their depressive cycle.

● A medical checkup is worthwhile. Some physical or biochemical disturbances can trigger depression. A change in diet or some temporary medication may be just what the doctor ordered.

● Sometimes depression requires professional counseling help. About 12 percent of depressed persons withdraw socially or become suicidal. Upsets of this magnitude warrant getting immediate professional support.

● Depression is a faith question. Persons who become depressed are usually pessimistic about life now, but religious faith reminds us we can be optimistic about the long term. God is in control ultimately. Like the song says, "He's got the whole world in his hands."

Blues, Stay Away from Me

Sermon Text: Psalm 118:24

An emotionally disturbed man went to see a noted psychiatrist. He confessed he was frustrated, depressed, and desperate. The psychiatrist probed. Finally, after a lengthy consultation, the psychiatrist remembered there was a circus in town. He recommended the troubled man go see the circus clown. The psychiatrist said, "He will make you laugh, and you will feel better." The disturbed man blurted out, "But doctor, I am the clown!" Each of us, even the clown, is subject to periods of depression and blues. "Blues stay away from me" is the prayer of every depressed soul.

Psalm 118 tells us how to drive the blues away. This is one of the great hymns of the ancient Psalter, an individual's hymn of thanksgiving. This can be seen in verses 5-19,21, and 28. Some commentators think this psalm was written by Hezekiah after his serious illness. The fifth verse gives us some keen insight into this psalm. The Revised Standard Version more accurately translates verse 5, "Out of my distress I called on the Lord;/

the Lord answered me and set me free." The Lord has the ability to set us free. He not only has the ability to set us free from physical ailments and our enemies, but he can also set us free from our depressions.

All of us get the blues at times. No one is sure what causes the blues, but many of us blame life's circumstances. For example, one depressed fellow said, "I went to a restaurant last night. When I asked the waiter for a fork, he told me I'd have to wait, because somebody else was using it. Finally, when I ordered a hot cocoa, he brought me a chocolate bar and a match."

Another man was depressed because of a traffic ticket. He said, "I have the worst lawyer in the world. I was in court with a simple traffic violation. When I asked my lawyer how to plead, he said, 'On your knees.'"

The circumstance of retirement brings depression to some people. One man who had a bad case of blues right after he retired was moaning about his company being very cheap. He said, "At my company you get the gold watch when you retire, but you only get to keep it until the next guy retires."

One depressed ecologist complained about the rate at which we are slaughtering our wildlife. He said, "It is not going to be long before the forests are going to have to buy their animals from the pet shops."

Obviously, the circumstances of our lives contribute to our blues, but they are not the primary factor in our depression. Andrew Lester in his book *It Hurts So Bad, Lord!* (Broadman Press, © 1976) says there are three primary causes of depression. He believes anger is a significant contributing factor to depression, particularly among Christians. For so long we have taught it is unchristian to express anger that many people experience anger and suppress it. If you suppress anger long enough, it causes depression.

Lester believes guilt is another major cause of depression. Guilt tends to generate a sense of shame and a feeling of worthlessness within us. When our conscience is violated, when we feel we have transgressed our basic value system, the result is guilt. When our guilt is not resolved, we begin to feel bad about ourselves. We worry about what other people think of us. We feel we have been unfaithful to our basic commitments. We experience shame. We feel inadequate, incapable, undeserving. We develop low self-esteem, not believing we are worth anything to anybody. Depression results.

Dr. Lester also believes grief contributes to depression. He says, "When we experience the loss of something which has been of significance, the result is grief." Any kind of loss or separation can shake the foundations of meaning in our life, call our faith into question, disturb our perceptions of life, make us feel both anger and guilt, and bring on many self-doubts and self-criticisms. Any or all of these can lead to depression.

What can we do about depression? Some people try to ignore it, thinking it will go away. Others try to drive it away by going on drinking binges or spending sprees. Many people try to deal with their depression by seeking thrills, but thrill seeking is not an effective long-term method for dealing with our blues. Thrill seeking is simply a more sophisticated way of suppressing depression.

How can you as a Christian take positive practical steps in keeping the blues away? First, begin by reviewing your theology.

Recently in East Hartford, Connecticut, an ex-convict held nearly one hundred policemen at bay for sixteen hours in a barricaded, second-floor apartment. He then killed his wife and son and shot himself to death. Frank DeCorleta, a thirty-four-year-old ex-Georgia prisoner, apparently took his own life rather than go back to prison. In a telephone interview with a local newspaper during the siege, DeCorleta said, "God hates me. Life is terrible. It stinks." DeCorleta gave us a great deal of insight into his depression by his theology. He said, "God hates me." That kind of theology can cause serious depression.

Compare that kind of theology with the theology found in

Psalm 118:1,5-6,22-23. One commentator feels no one less than
a great composer can do justice to this psalm. Linguists and
historians can help by explaining obscure words and phrases,
but a musical genius is needed to help us see what the
psalmist may have seen, a company of pilgrims or victorious
warriors marching toward Zion's hill. Whether they are intent
upon military celebrations or religious festivals, there is order
in their movements, and they sing as they advance. A voice
announces the theme: "O give thanks unto the Lord; for he is
good," and the full choir immediately responds, "because his
mercy endureth for ever." Again, a solitary voice is uplifted in
the words, "Let Israel now say," and again the refrain is
repeated by the chorus, "that his mercy endureth for ever." The
theme is repeated first to the whole nation, then to the priests,
finally to proselytes young and old; and every phrase prompts
the united response, "His mercy endureth for ever." The
psalmist's theology was obvious: God is good, and he loves
men. If we approach life with the concept that God hates us,
we will surely get depressed.

The psalmist says, "I called upon the Lord in distress: the
Lord answered me, and set me in a large place. The Lord is on
my side; I will not fear: what can man do unto me?" (vv. 5-6). If
we approach life with the understanding that God is on our
side, that he loves us, that "his mercy endureth for ever," then
we will not be struck with feelings of inadequacies, self-pity,
and a sense of worthlessness. A great deal of depression is
caused by the fact that we don't think God cares about us.

The Bible says, "The stone which the builders refused is
become the head stone of the corner. This is the Lord's doing; it
is marvellous in our eyes" (vv. 22-23). The psalmist points out
that despised people have become an honorable nation under
God. This verse is referred to several times in the New
Testament. It is popularly applied to Christ who was rejected
by the Jews and became the very foundation for the kingdom
of God. The psalmist was confident that God makes no mis-
takes, that God can even use the bad circumstances of life, like

the death of Christ, and turn them into good.

How do you view God? If you see him as an angry judge bent on getting back at you, the blues will settle on your doorstep. If you see God as the primary instigator of every event in life, then you will interpret life's bumps as God's punishment. Do you see every trouble that comes your way as God disciplining you? If that's the case, then your self-esteem will degenerate to zero, and blues will be impossible to shake. When you are depressed, it may be that you are down on yourself because you wrongly believe God is punishing you for something. If you believe God is love and cares for you, the blues will lose their grip on your life.

How do you view God? When you get depressed, review your theology. Ask yourself, *Do I believe he is a God of love, that he is good, and his mercy endures forever toward me?*

Second, to banish the blues, renew your faith. You can renew your faith by realizing God is more trustworthy than men or nations. The psalmist said, "It is better to trust in the Lord than to put confidence in man. It is better to trust in the Lord than to put confidence in princes" (vv. 8-9). Anytime we put faith in men, they have the possibility of disappointing us. We cannot put our security in nations or princes, for they rise and fall. But the God of creation who made us will relate to us faithfully forever. We can trust him, so we must renew our faith in him.

We also can renew our faith in him by remembering what good things he has done for us. A casual reading of verses 10-14 indicates the psalmist may have been a prince of Israel whose kingdom was threatened by Gentile attackers. He gave God the credit for delivering him. He was grateful to God.

The psalmist says, "I shall not die, but live, and declare the works of the Lord. The Lord hath chastened me sore: but he hath not given me over unto death" (vv. 17-18). This psalm describes King Hezekiah who was smitten with a grave illness, but the psalmist makes it clear that it was God who delivered him from his illness. The psalmist is simply looking back at his life and seeing how good God had been to him. He renewed his faith as he counted his blessings.

Martin Luther gives us some great insights into this psalm. Luther spent a period of solitude at Coburg studying this psalm and writing a commentary upon it. When the work was completed, Luther dedicated it to Abbot Friedrich and sent it to him saying that of all his possessions, he had concluded that it was the best he could give. Luther said:

> This is my psalm, my chosen psalm. I love them all; I love all Holy Scripture, which is my consolation and my life. But this psalm is nearest my heart, and I have a familiar right to call it mine. It has saved me from many a pressing danger, from which nor emperor, nor kings, nor sages, nor saints could have saved me. It is my friend; dearer to me than all the honors and power of earth.[1]

Luther had been threatened by secular princes and military powers. He was threatened by the Roman Catholic Church. He was disappointed by some of his friends who took the Reformation in a different direction. In later life he struggled with ill health, but he also recalled the goodness of God and renewed his faith. As you renew your faith, you can drive the blues away.

In Psalm 37:5 the Bible says, "Commit thy way unto the Lord; trust also in him; and he shall bring it to pass." Most of us have a problem knowing how to commit our ways unto the Lord and trust in him. How do you translate that into everyday life? How do you trust in the Lord when you are depressed? How do you commit your way unto the Lord when you have the blues? I believe faith is acting as though something is, even if every evidence indicates it is not. Faith is living as if you will get well when the medical diagnosis says otherwise. Faith is giving 10 percent of your earnings to the Lord when your checkbook says you can't live on 90 percent of what you make. Faith is sharing your personal testimony with people you are afraid will reject you. Faith is trusting your teenager again after your teenager has been proven untrustworthy. Faith is living with the attitude that your life is OK when the outward circumstances indicates it is not OK. Faith is committing your depression to the Lord and living as though you are not depressed. Psychologists might say you are suppressing your depression or living out of touch with reality when you do that. I like to think I'm transferring my depression. I simply transfer it to God and let him do with it as he may. I believe he is big enough to handle my depressions and do with them whatever he likes. When you get depressed, exercise faith. Transfer your depression to God.

Third, you can drive the blues away by rechanneling your energy.

Verse 24 is the high-water mark of this psalm. The psalmist came to see that "This is the day which the Lord has made" (RSV). He had decided he was going to rejoice and be glad in the present. His change of attitude is seen in verse 26 when he said, "Blessed be he that cometh in the name of the Lord: we have blessed you out of the house of the Lord." The psalmist now saw life as good because he saw God as good. The psalmist decided he was going to approach life with a positive spirit. Jesus displayed the same attitude in Matthew 5:38-44. The Bible says that as a man "thinketh in his heart, so is he" (Prov. 23:7). If we think negative and depressing thoughts, we will be negative and depressed people. We must rechannel our thoughts and our energies. Paul said Christians are to let the same mind be in us which is in Christ. We are to be filled with all the fullness of God. All of this means we should rid ourselves of the garbage in our lives and replace it with the good things of God. We must rechannel our thoughts and our energies.

Majorie Van Ouwerkerk quit teaching when her youngest daughter left for college. She hadn't sufficiently recuperated from an operation in time for the start of the school. She began to find herself inert, uncaring, and disinterested. She lost her sense of humor and began to wallow in self-pity. She went to see a doctor, who advised her to start exercising vigorously. She bought a pedometer and pinned it to her slacks to check the distance, put a leash on her dog, and started walking each morning right after breakfast. She was committed to walking every morning, rain, shine, or snow. She started on her journey each morning by quoting the verse, "This is the day which the Lord hath made; we will rejoice and be glad in it" (Ps. 118:24). Everytime a sad thought crept in she would repeat that verse. She started praying as she walked. She started silently blessing everyone she met. She started thanking God for her health and the beauty of the morning. She started feeling better and started making her walks longer and longer. Her prayer life deepened as she became more aware of the presence of God on her walks. Since her daughter was now in college and didn't need her energy, she rechanneled her energy and began exercising.

I've never talked with a person who exercised regularly and vigorously who was attacked by long periods of depression. All of us have the blues occasionally, but if we will rechannel our energy and get on a vigorous exercise program, our blues will not last as long. I don't suggest you stop with rechanneling your physical energy. Rechannel your mental energy too. Don't read depressing materials. Don't see depressing movies. Don't fill your mind with depressing materials, or you will think depressing thoughts. Most of all, rechannel your spiritual energy. Don't spend your spiritual energy condemning people, gossiping, wrecking the character of others. Give away your spiritual energy by blessing everyone you meet. Look for the good in people. Trust people. Encourage people. Brag on people. Expect the best of people, and in so doing you will drive the blues away from your door and theirs, too.

Note

1. Martin Luther, Prothero, *Psalms in Human Life*, p. 94.

4

When to Cleanse Temples

Anger is a powerful emotion and simmers just below the surface in many people. Eugene Ionesco's chilling parable *Anger* reveals the low boiling point of our modern world. This short play takes place on a beautiful Sunday in a beautiful, country town. Wives are complimented and beggars are even rewarded generously in this idyllic setting. Then, the mood changes across the town as one after another the husbands discover flies in their soup. Complaints turn into insults. Bowls are smashed, and soup runs under doors into the streets. Domestic arguments escalate into a small-town riot and finally into a nuclear holocaust. The planet is blown up because of a fly in a bowl of soup. Ionesco's point is frighteningly clear: When unleashed, anger's chain reactions can get out of control and become destructive.

The Roots of Anger

Have you ever wondered where anger comes from? There are lots of theories hinting at the roots of anger. One approach suggests a defective gene, a bad seed, causes some people to become criminals. Another theory says anger and violence strengthen society by weeding out weaker persons. For example, President Theodore Roosevelt described the Spanish-American War as a "moral tonic." Animal observers raise a third possibility. They note

animals fight over territory, status, and mates and claim
humans do the same. One psychologist sees a key difference between animals and humans, however: "Animals
don't fight over politics and religion." Freud had yet another explanation for anger and hostility. He theorized
opposing drives in man—one toward life and health, the
other toward death and destruction. Anger, according to
Freud, expresses itself either destructively in aggression,
war, and suicide or constructively in healthy goals and
changing society for the good. From a Christian perspective, human sinfulness and selfishness are basic triggers for
our anger. Each of these theories may give us some clues to
our personal anger.

American culture reflects a great deal of anger. Over
twenty thousand Americans are shot to death with
handguns yearly. Television programs are violent, too. For
instance, by age eighteen the average American youngster
will have viewed more than eighteen thousand murders on
TV. Even economics plays a role in our expressions of anger.
When cotton prices went down and jobs became scarce in
the South, lynchings became more numerous. Almost five
thousand occurred in the United States between 1880 and
1930. Hard times often cause anger to build up and explode.

Wherever our anger comes from, we all know how it feels
to be angry. Medical researchers tell us several bodily
reactions occur when anger ignites:

- Heart beat increases.
- Blood supplies switch from digestive processes to the
  heart, nervous system, and muscles.
- Sugar reserves are released by the liver.
- Blood pressure rises.
- Respiration deepens.
- The spleen enriches the blood.
- Adrenalin is secreted.

Our bodies automatically convert to a ready state when we

become angry. In spite of all these physical and chemical signals, some folks claim they never get angry.

Jesus and Anger

Many people think Christians don't or shouldn't feel anger. Aren't Christians supposed to be loving persons? After all, the early church listed anger as one of the seven deadly sins, we reason. Therefore, when Christians feel their anger well up, they may either deny their feelings or simply feel guilty for being angry.

Some occasions justified Jesus' anger. (1) He was angered by indifference to human need. Early in his ministry Jesus observed a man with a withered hand worshiping in the synagogue. The Pharisees were offended at Jesus' sensitivity to the crippled man's obvious need. Only medical emergencies were allowed treatment on the sabbath. The man's injury would "keep until tomorrow," according to the Pharisee's logic. Notice Jesus' angry reaction: "And he looked around at them with anger, grieved at their hardness of heart, and said to the man, 'Stretch out your hand.' He stretched it out, and his hand was restored" (Mark 3:5, RSV). When the needs of persons were deliberately ignored, Jesus became angry.

(2) Jesus was also angered by sick religion. When he cleansed the Temple, Jesus demonstrated his deep indignation at cheating and exploiting people in the name of religion. The money changer's practices and the Pharisees' attitudes made worship less accessible to common people (Matt. 21:10-17). Jesus didn't cleanse the Temple while singing "There's a Sweet, Sweet Spirit in This Place." He was genuinely angry at bad religion.

Christians are justified in feeling and expressing anger. Jesus did. When we confront hard hearts and unhealthy churches, our anger will boil up as our Lord's did. Anger under such circumstances is predictable and rightly grounded.

Taming Our Anger

Anger can be channeled constructively. Paul instructed Christians to "Be angry but do not sin" (Eph. 4:26, RSV). Obviously, Paul felt anger could be expressed positively. In fact, Paul gives one guideline for constructive conflict as he continues: "Do not let the sun go down on your anger" (Eph. 4:26, RSV). Staying up-to-date on venting our anger is a good rule to follow.

Anger is like a horse. Either it can be wild, unbridled, and unmanageable, or anger can be controlled, channeled, and used for constructive purposes. The challenge for the Christian is to tame and direct his anger, to master anger rather than be overpowered and destroyed by it. Several actions help us tame our anger:

- Learn to count to ten. In other words, give yourself a chance to cool off before you pop off.
- Talk out your anger. Even strong emotions like anger shrink when we put them in words. Talking out our anger is a healthy release.
- Exercise vigorously when you're angry. Run or play off your anger. This is a safer method for blowing off steam than saying or doing something you'll regret later.
- When depressed, look for bottled up anger. The "blues" are often triggered by anger turned in upon ourselves. Anger can be released and must be, or we'll pay a physical, emotional, and spiritual price.
- Remember anger is natural. Recognize your anger and look for safe ways to express it.
- Watch for patterns in your anger. If you boil over often, a physical exam may help you discover fatigue, chemical imbalances, or other ailments making you edgy. Don't be ashamed to share your anger patterns with a

counselor or other persons specially trained to help you understand these patterns and their sources.

- Don't hesitate to confront God. Some anger is felt toward God. When this type of anger is experienced, talk and pray to God until you sense a breakthrough in this crucial relationship. Our honest expression of our needs to our Heavenly Father can open the door to new dimensions of faith and steps of service.

Can a Christian Express Anger?

Sermon Text: John 2:13-17

The great maestro Toscanini was as well known for his ferocious temper as for his outstanding musicianship. When members of his orchestra played badly, he would pick up anything in sight and hurl it to the floor. During one rehearsal a flat note caused the genius to grab his valuable watch and smash it. Shortly afterward, his devoted musicians gave him a luxurious, velvet-lined box containing two watches, one a beautiful gold timepiece, the other a cheap one on which was inscribed "For rehearsals only." That very clever incident carries a timeless truth: There is a time and a place for expressing anger.

The Old Testament makes you immediately aware of God's anger. He drove Adam and Eve out because of his anger at their sin. He poured out his wrath upon the earth and destroyed it because of the sin in the day of Noah. He destroyed the cities of Sodom and Gomorrah because of sin. Because of his anger, he replaced Saul as king. Turn to Nahum 1:2-6 and read of the anger of God.

The New Testament pictures Jesus as meek and compassionate, but this doesn't mean he was weakly good-natured. Those who knew Jesus best remembered that his eyes could become like a flame and his breath as hot as a furnace (Mark 3:5). There was nothing mild in that fierce message he sent to Herod (Luke 13:32, RSV) when he said, "Go and tell that fox." Nor were there any traces of mildness in him when he turned upon his friend Peter, who had meant only kindness, and with that terrific rebuke said, "Get thee behind me, Satan" (Matt. 16:23). The Pharisees did not find him gentle, meek, or mild when he pursued them with those blistering denunciations: "You white-washed tombs, you serpents, you make him, your proselyte, twice as much a child of hell as yourselves" (Matt. 23:15,27,33, writer's paraphrase). When Jesus went to the Temple and found traders polluting the Temple of God, he expressed anger again.

Many of us Christians have been taught, either by implication or overtly, that it is unchristian to get angry. That attitude may be the cause of many problems in Christian churches. Perhaps you and I would be healthier human beings if we were convinced that a wholesome expression of anger is not only good for us but godly.

A Virginia woman with a fiery temper died. They were having her funeral when a storm arose. Just as they lowered her casket the wind began to blow and roll. Lightning struck frighteningly close by. Her husband quickly looked heaven-ward and said, "She has arrived." I like his theology. If God in heaven is capable of anger, then we are capable of it also.

The Bible makes it clear God expressed his anger. Jesus, God incarnate, expressed anger too. We who are made in the image of God are justified in expressing anger. The question is, What are the guidelines for the Christian to use in knowing when and how to express anger?

First, anger is justified when there is injustice. The Passover was the greatest Jewish feast. Every adult male Jew who lived within twenty miles of Jerusalem was required to attend, but it was not just the Jews in Palestine who came. By John's day the Jews were scattered widely but hadn't forgotten their ancestral faith and land. It was the dream of every Jew to celebrate at least one Passover in Jerusalem. Sometimes as many as 2¼ million Jews came to the Holy City for the event. Every Jew over nineteen years old had to pay the Temple tax. This tax of a half shekel was used to support the Temple. A half shekel was equivalent to almost two days' wages.

All kinds of currencies were used in Jerusalem at that time, but the Temple tax had to be paid in Galilean shekels, the coin of the sanctuary. So when pilgrims from other parts of the world came to Passover with their foreign coins, their money had to be changed into Jewish currency before it could be given for the Temple tax. The money changers in the Temple were making at least 33 percent on their investment when they exchanged foreign currency. What enraged Jesus was that the pilgrims to the Passover, who could least afford it, were being fleeced by the money changers.

But that was not all. There were also people who sold oxen, sheep, and doves for sacrifice. Many pilgrims wished to offer a thanksgiving offering for their journey to the Holy City. Many of them could not bring a sacrifice on their long journey. They had to buy a sacrificial animal after they arrived. The Law stated the animal sacrifices had to be perfect, flawless, and unblemished. The Temple authorities had appointed inspectors to examine the victims to be offered. The inspectors were paid by the worshipers for their inspection. If a worshiper brought a victim from outside the Temple, it was almost certain the victim would be examined and rejected. Then the worshiper would be forced to buy a sacrifice from those who sold the sacrifices within the Temple, and, of course, they sold the sacrificial animals at a ridiculously high price.

These two issues moved Jesus to flaming anger. John's Gospel tells us Jesus took cords and made a whip. He could not stand idly by and see such injustice. It is right to express anger when injustice is being practiced.

One of my high school classmates came to our twentieth high school reunion with a "whip" in her hand. There was a time in our program for everyone to tell what he or she had been doing for the last twenty years. We were all anxious to hear from Pat. It was rumored she had moved to California and married Paul Newman's brother. When she stood to tell about her past twenty years, she cleansed a temple. She said, "I have not been back to Oklahoma in the last twenty years and probably will not come back until you do something about letting women become human beings." She got on her soapbox and preached in favor of the Equal Rights Amendment. She accused the state of Oklahoma of being backward and generally offended the residents of the state and most of her classmates. She went about accomplishing her purposes very awkwardly, but she did remind me of one truth: Injustice is being practiced in most of our society against women.

With a growing daughter who will someday be a woman, I am more uniquely aware of the fact that women are not paid as well for their work as a man who works beside them. Women are victims of injustices regarding credit, Social Security, and insurance. Perhaps we need to get angry regarding the social injustices against women, children, and minorities.

Second, anger is justified when religion is abused. A number of times in the Old Testament the issue of the relevance of animal sacrifice in religion was raised (Isa. 1:11; Hos. 8:13; Ps. 51:16). Prophetic voices before Jesus had been telling men of the sheer irrelevancy and irreverence of the burnt offerings and the animal sacrifices which smoked continuously upon the altar at Jerusalem. Maybe Jesus acted as he did to show that no sacrifice alone of any animal could ever put a man into right relationship with God. Jesus might very well have run the money changers out of the Temple because he saw in their practice an abuse of religion. How much evil is perpetrated today in the name of religion?

A former minister of music came into my office one day obviously burdened. We chatted a few minutes, and then he shared his concern with me. A friend of my minister of music had just experienced some real tension in his marriage. As the minister of music in a large Southern Baptist church, the friend had not given his family the attention they needed. In an effort to get some attention, the man's wife left him. She went home to her family and indicated she might not come back. After several weeks the minister of music was approached by his pastor. His pastor said, "I have really been concerned about your marriage. I've been praying about it, and I really believe the Lord would not want you to serve his church without a wife. Therefore, I expect you to resign at our next business meeting." The man resigned, and his marriage did break up.

Let's take a look at the situation. The many hours this man spent serving the Lord through the local church contributed to his marital breakdown. It was not the sole cause but a contributing one. At a time in his life when he needed the support of his pastor and his church the most, they abandoned him; and the pastor did so in the name of religion. Had Jesus been present he might have had a whip in his hand.

We often abuse religion in training our children. How many times have you used God as a whip to get your children to do what you wanted them to do? How often is religion abused in athletics? How many times have people prayed that God will help them win a game? That kind of praying assumes God is one team's friend and the other team's enemy. I will confess to you I often get angry, and I believe God does, too, when people abuse religion.

Third, anger is justified when it is clearly motivated by love. Mark says something about the cleansing of the Temple which the other Gospel writers left out: "My house shall be called of all nations the house of prayer" (Mark 11:17). That phrase "of all nations" is Mark's unique contribution. The Temple consisted of a series of courts leading into the Temple proper and into the holy place. There was first the court of the Gentiles, then the court of the women, then the court of Israel, and then the court of the priests. All this buying and selling was going on out in the court of the Gentiles. The court of the Gentiles was the only place into which a Gentile might come. He had no access to the inner courts. So if a Gentile came into the court of the Gentiles to think, pray, and meditate, he could only distantly touch God. It was his only place of worship, and the Temple authorities and Jewish traders were making the court of the Gentiles into an uproar where no man could worship. All the noise literally shut out the seeking Gentiles from the presence of God. Jesus' love for the seeking Gentiles caused him to drive the money changers out of the Temple.

In a church I served formerly, our custodian resigned. A new Christian applied for the job. Our building committee hired him. He admitted knowing nothing about being a church custodian but said he was willing to learn. It would be a good environment for him to work in as he grew in faith. Honestly, he didn't do a very good job. I began to bear down on him. He started doing better work, but he and the chairman of the building committee had a personality clash. One night I passed the church, and I saw a light flicker inside the building. I got out of my car and went inside, fearing I might meet a burglar. I went to the room where I had seen the light and found the chairman of our building committee down on the floor with a flashlight trying to spot dust. He was looking for accusations to bring against our custodian. I immediately asked him to turn in his keys and resign as chairman of the committee. True, our custodian had not been doing a good job, but I knew more was at stake than a custodial position. We had a babe in Christ on our hands. If we fired him without giving him a fair chance, he might be lost to the kingdom of God. He would remain a babe in Christ the rest of his life. Because of my love for this young Christian, I was angry.

It is not healthy to lose control of yourself and be a slave to your temper. Neither is it healthy to experience hostility or anger and bottle it up. Many people who become emotionally ill are religious people who have been taught all of their lives that it is unchristian to get angry. It is unchristian to experience anger and not admit it. It may also be unchristian to express every feeling of anger that comes your way. But if your anger is motivated by love and a genuine concern for the welfare of the recipient of your anger, then express it.

A few years ago a rather unusual announcement was repeated over the radio. The announcer gave several scenes in this progressive history of a person. Scene one showed a crying baby and a proud father. The father was saying, "Oh, it's a boy. It's a boy. We're going to name him Stanley, and one day he will become the president of the United States." In scene two Stanley was getting married. At Stanley's wedding the father of the bride was saying to Stanley, "Oh, I know you would like to go to medical school, son, but you are going to join me in the purse manufacturing business." In the third scene, Stanley and his wife were on an expensive vacation. He obviously had been a successful manufacturer and had made a lot of money. The final scene showed Stanley's minister preaching his funeral. The minister said, "Stanley was much beloved by all those who lived here at the Shady Nook Rest Home. He was the best gin rummy player in Shady Nook, and a few people knew that he also had the lowest cholesterol count of anyone here." Then the announcer on the radio said, "Isn't it sad to live your whole life and never make a ripple and never rock a boat? Join the Peace Corps." Isn't it sad to live your whole life and never make a ripple or rock a boat or cleanse a temple?

5

I Worry Enough for Everyone

Worry is America's national addiction. Inflation, choles-terol, pollution, weather, recession, fuel shortages, math tests, aging, airplane safety, Social Security, overweight, taxes, acne, unemployment, in-laws, blue Mondays, mean bosses, rainy weekends, inferiority complexes—choose any two and worry yourself silly. Worry's only function is to fill up our time and minds. We are obsessed by the imag-ined terrors of unknown futures.

Poet W. H. Auden called our time the "age of anxiety." Others see ours as "the ulcer age," "the aspirin age," and "the rat race." Frank Kostyu notes worry's corrosive effect and calls it "the rust of life." Whatever we call it, lots of Americans are hooked on worry.

The Davenport Diagnosis

I worry enough for everyone most of the time. I call one of my worst episodes of worry "The Case of the Davenport Diagnosis." It happened while I was in seminary. During the spring I had a severe bout with the flu. Several weeks later I realized I still didn't have any pep. At this point worry took over. (I decided I was suffering from a recurrence of child-hood rheumatic fever. I was doomed—at least that's what my frightened innards kept telling me.)

For several days I wallowed in worry. Then I took action. One of the best internal medicine specialists in the South-west was a member of my church. Dr. Davenport was a respected diagnostic detective and was used widely as a medical consultant. After worship one Sunday morning I asked him for an examination. (In my fantasy I imagined he would rivet me with his professional gaze, see rigor mortis creeping in, and send me to the emergency room immediately.) In fact he said, "I'll be glad to examine you. Call my office in the morning and arrange an appointment."

My appointment was set for three weeks in the future. The time was an eternity in my mind. (I died a thousand deaths—all lingering, all more courageous than the martyrs. You'd be surprised how many fatal diseases you can imagine in three weeks.) At last the fateful day arrived. I put on my best suit (and wondered if it was fit to bury a terminally ill twenty-five-year-old preacher in). Every step to the doctor's office took supreme effort. (I only hoped I wouldn't linger on in terrible pain.)

Dr. Davenport was thorough, and his nurses were kind. All morning long they listened, sampled, probed, and tested. Finally, Dr. Davenport called me in. (I settled into a chair determined to be brave and hear my sentence with the valor of Daniel in the lion's den.) Quietly, Dr. Davenport told me I was as healthy as a horse and was now completely over the aftereffects of the flu.

I went home feeling healthy and energetic for the first time in weeks. The Davenport diagnosis had cured me. (The bill for the examination was the final proof I'd better get back to work!) As any good physician knows, 90 percent of the cure is in the proper diagnosis. Dr. Davenport discovered my only illness was anxiety. I'd worried myself sick. Can you identify with my experience?

Faith or Worry

Faith crowds out worry. The theological reason is obvious. When we become anxious, we have two options: We can either depend on God or try to go it alone. It's an either-or proposition, not both-and. For the Christian, happy living is by faith alone, not faith and worry.

Reinhold Niebuhr called anxiety the precondition of sin. He pictured a sailor climbing the mast of a sailing ship. Suspended in such a worrisome situation, anxiety sets in. Worry, then, sets the stage for faith or sin depending on our choice of either faith in God or more worry.

Niebuhr's belief that worry preconditions sin led him to compose a famous prayer: "God, give us grace to accept with serenity the things that cannot be changed, courage to change the things which should be changed, and the wisdom to distinguish one from the other." That's a prayer for the worrier.

Surviving the Rat Race

Other suggestions for dealing with worry include:

• Separate your past from the future. Worrying about your past poisons today—so isolate past from present. Don't blame today's problems on how your parents treated you as a child or on Adam's sin. Yesterday's gone forever. Forget it and live today now.

• Recognize that life isn't a rose garden. Don't expect to live without a little frustration, tension, or anger. Remember we win some, lose some, and have some rained out. So don't worry when life isn't all perfection and success.

• Enjoy what you have. If you're blessed with good health, enjoy it, and protect it. Don't worry about what you'd do if you had a heart attack. Over 90 percent of our worries never come true, so stop and smell the roses.

• Live with your limits. Don't fuss with God or yourself because you're not as smart as Einstein or as musical as Bach. You're only responsible for your talents and your own life. Accept whatever realistic limits you have, and don't push yourself beyond your limits.

• Fly as high as God allows. A pilot heard a gnawing

sound in his small plane while aloft over the South Pacific. Instantly he realized a giant island rat was aboard with him and could chew through some vital part of the aircraft. The pilot knew he was at least two hours away from the nearest landing strip. How could he rid his plane of his rodent stowaway? Suddenly, he knew the solution to his dilemma. Putting on his oxygen mask, he put his plane into a climb. Up the plane climbed through fourteen thousand, sixteen thousand, eighteen thousand, twenty thousand, to twenty-five thousand feet. The gnawing sound stopped. Two hours later, after landing, the pilot found the rat dead, unable to live at such a high altitude. Faith encourages high flight in life situations. Let God, not worry, determine your ultimate levels of service and performance.

You Can Do My Worrying

Sermon Text: Matthew 6:25-34

On two occasions in my life I have been worried to the point I had difficulty sleeping. My first experience was in the spring of 1966. My retarded brother was living with us. I was in my mid-twenties and far too young to have a retarded teenager as my responsibility. I was also trying to get into graduate school and under a lot of pressure while making preparations for the entrance exams. I was studying until after midnight almost every night and waking up at three or four o'clock in the morning unable to go back to sleep. I would lie in bed and worry about the things ahead of me.

My second terrible experience with worry was in the spring of 1968. At age twenty-seven I was the new pastor of one of the largest churches in northwest Arkansas. It was a larger church than I had ever dreamed of serving. I wanted so desperately to do well. I was also in graduate school, flying back and forth from northwest Arkansas to Dallas-Fort Worth.

There were several tensions in the church that always go along with a change in leadership. On the day Martin Luther King, Jr., was killed, I went into the home of one of our members for a visit. As soon as I walked in, this full-blooded, Choctaw Indian woman said to me, "Well, that 'nigger' finally got what was coming to him." Just a few minutes before, I had been sitting in front of our television weeping as I watched the reports of his murder. What she said angered me. Her own parents had been discriminated against racially in Oklahoma. Now she was exhibiting one of the worst racial attitudes I had ever seen. After I got home I realized how angrily I had reacted to her. I worried about what she would say to other members of the congregation. I envisioned professional failure in my first opportunity in a good church. For several weeks I had great difficulty sleeping because of worry. Through that experience I came to discover the uselessness of worry and decided to let someone else do my worrying for me.

"Worry" describes a feeling of anxiety, trouble, or uneasiness. Jesus spoke of worry when he said, "Take no thought for your life" (Matt. 6:25). The word translated "Take no thought" literally means "don't worry anxiously." Jesus wasn't forbidding foresight or advocating reckless thoughtlessness. He was advocating a freedom from the anxiety that possesses our lives when we worry. He knew that worry did no good at all and advocated that his followers let someone else do their worrying for them.

If you're looking for something to worry about, you'll always find it. You can worry about finances, family, friends, or health.

We can worry about the uncertainty of life itself, or the lack of control we have over our own destiny. Many of us work ourselves to death trying to get into a responsible position, and then we worry ourselves to death about all the responsibility we have. Some people even worry a great deal about the weather.

You can do my worrying because worry is an indictment against my faith. Jesus said,

> Take no thought for your life, what ye shall eat, or what ye shall drink; nor yet for your body, what ye shall put on. Is not the life more than meat, and the body than raiment? Behold the fowls of the air: for they sow not, neither do they reap, nor gather into barns; yet your heavenly Father feedeth them. Are ye not much better than they? (Matt. 6:25-26).

Jesus points out that God is the one who has given us life. If God gave us life, then surely we can trust him to sustain it. Jesus reminds us that God takes care of the birds. They don't worry or attempt to store up goods for unforeseeable tragedies, yet their lives go on. The point here is not that the birds don't work, rather that we should trust that God loves us and is going to take care of us. In verses 28-32 Jesus made reference to the lilies: "Wherefore, if God so clothe the grass of the field, which to-day is and to-morrow is cast into the oven." The beautiful flowers that decorated the hillsides of Palestine bloomed one day and were burned up by the Palestinian heat the next. If God loves the short-lived flower, how much more does he love us, the highest of all his creation?

The crux of what Jesus is saying is almost hidden in the parentheses of verse 32. Here is the strongest argument against worry. Worry is characteristic of one who doesn't know God. The heathens believed in a God who hated them or at least a God who was often angry with them. The heathen basically distrusted their God. Jesus reveals to us a different kind of God. We have a God who loves and cares for us. If we worry, we issue an indictment against God.

Insurance companies must hire some great psychologists. Have you ever noticed how they manage to put their flight insurance at just the right places in airports? The first time my wife and I traveled abroad was in 1970. We were in and out of three air terminals before we finally boarded our international plane. All I saw that day were flight insurance machines. When we were over the ocean an hour or so I entertained the thought, for a moment, about going down in the ocean. I'm sure those thoughts of doubt were placed there by those crazy insurance machines. The width of the ocean began to prey upon my mind. And then I chased those doubts away. I began to flood my mind with thoughts of God. I thought about God creating the ocean, giving man the intelligence to create a plane, and having the power to take care of me no matter where I was.

Worry is essentially irreligious. This does not mean that we can experience absolute serenity, that we can live all the time in perfect peace. But it does mean that we do not have to be a slave to worry. Your worry is an indictment against God's ability to care for you.

You can do my worrying because I have better things to do. Jesus asked, "Which of you by taking thought can add one cubit unto his stature?" (Matt. 6:27). This question had real significance to the small Jew. He was a head shorter than most of the Roman soldiers. Many Jews tried desperately to stretch themselves to a greater height so they wouldn't have to look up to their Roman masters. Although they might worry over their shortness, there was no way they could add the desired height by worrying. The point? Worrying is pointless, futile. You and I have better things to do. Jesus also said, "But seek ye first the kingdom of God, and his righteousness; and all these things shall be added unto you" (Matt. 6:33). To concentrate upon doing the will of God is the surest way to defeat worry. Jesus was convinced worry could be banished when the dominating power and love of God became our own consuming passion.

If you don't have anything better to do than worry, you need something new to do. Worry will make you miserable, give you high blood pressure, peptic ulcers, hypertension, and various mental illnesses. Worry can make you antisocial, cause you to distrust everyone, and rob you of your faith in yourself, other people, and God. And I don't know of a single good it can do. I've got better things to do than to worry, so I'm going to let you do my worrying for me.

You can do my worrying for me because I can stop worrying by dividing life into manageable blocks. Jesus said, "Take therefore no thought for the morrow: for the morrow shall take thought for the things of itself. Sufficient unto the day is the evil thereof" (Matt. 6:34). This is essentially a warning against borrowing tomorrow's troubles for today. Jesus is warning us against burdening today with worry over the unknown problems of tomorrow. We can destroy ourselves with anxiety over a future we cannot control. Only God knows the future. If we trust in him, the future will be taken care of by him. Besides, we have no certainty of tomorrow. Worry burdens us down when we begin to live life in too large a chunk; but when we begin to break life down into manageable pieces, we can conquer worry. Let's break life down into pieces we can handle.

In his sermon entitled "How to Worry," Ralph Phelps tells about the clock that had a nervous breakdown. This new clock was ticking away on the shelf two ticks to the second as any good, self-respecting clock should tick when it began to think about how many times it was going to have to tick. *Two ticks to the second means 120 ticks per minute, it mused. That's 7,200 ticks per hour; 172,800 ticks per day; 1,209,600 per week for 52 weeks; and a total of 62,899,200 ticks per year. Horrors!* Straightway the clock had a nervous breakdown. The clock was taken to a psychiatrist who patched up the mainspring as well as he could and then asked, "Clock, what's your trouble?" "Oh, doctor," wailed the clock, "I have to tick so much. I have to tick two ticks to the second and 120 ticks per minute and 7,200 ticks per hour, and . . ." "Hold it," the psychiatrist cut in. "How many ticks do you have to tick at a time?" "Oh, I just have to tick one at a time," was the reply. "Then let me make a suggestion," replied the doctor. "You go home and try ticking one tick at a time. Don't even think about the next tick until you get this tick ticked. I believe you'll improve rapidly." That was twenty years ago, and the clock is still ticking perfectly, one tick at a time. We need to learn the secret of breaking life down into chunks that we can manage.

What are the worry thoughts that occupy your mind? Are most of them concerned with what's going to happen tomorrow? You can do nothing about tomorrow. Break life down into manageable sizes. Yesterday is gone; forget about it. Tomorrow has not gotten here yet; don't worry with it. Today is here; live it!

Pick out two days every week you are not going to worry about. The first day you should not worry about is yesterday. Yesterday was yours, but now it is God's. Give it back to him and don't worry with it. The other day of the week you should not worry about is tomorrow. It is not yours yet, if it ever will be. It also belongs to God. Give it to him. If you will not worry about yesterday or tomorrow you will not likely worry much about today. Break life down into manageable chunks, and you can let someone else do your worrying for you.

II

ENCOURAGEMENT FOR CRISIS TIMES

6

A Time to Die

One day a group of people will go to a cemetery, hold a burial service, and go to their homes again. All except one: you. That cold fact will eventually be truth for all of us. As the Bible asserts with its balanced wisdom, "There is a right time for everything: A time to be born, a time to die" (Eccl. 3:1-2, TLB).

Everyone dies. Roughly 1 percent of the United States' population dies yearly. On the average, Americans experience a bereavement every six years. Widows outnumber widowers and average only fifty-six years of age.

American attitudes toward death are slowly changing. D-E-A-D is no longer considered a pornographic word. However, we in the United States still make attempts to deny death's reality by ignoring the language of death and trying to make dead persons attractive.

Grief's Pilgrimage

Grief, death's aftermath, is a process. Three distinct phases can be expected in grief.

• Shock. The impact of death is numbed by shock and unreality. We can't believe a loved one is gone. We can't understand what our loss means yet.

How can we help each other when grief is fresh? A ministry of presence—just being there—is important. You may not have words to say, but a speech is secondary at this stage anyway. As the contemporary card reads, "Don't just say something. Stand there."

I asked one hundred senior adult men, all leaders in their congregations, what the most helpful ministry of their pastors had been when their wives died. They agreed: "Just being there." And the least helpful act? Again, they agreed: "He talked too much." These church leaders believed in their pastors and in the words their pastors spoke; but when people are in shock, words don't sink in. In fact, words may intrude and irritate. Just being there is usually enough.

● Emotions overflow. We feel guilty: "Why didn't I do more?" We feel angry: "Why did God take her away from me?" We weep like Jesus did when his friend Lazarus died (John 11:35).

"Grief work," as the experts describe the pilgrimage of working through our loss, ordinarily takes about six months and requires six to ten hours of open discussion of the deceased with a caring listener to put our lives in perspective. Our ministry to each other in grief calls for lots of availability and quiet listening.

● Readjustment. After the shock and as our emotions work themselves out, we begin to adjust our lives without our dead loved one. Two errors are common in our encouragement of bereaved friends. First, we in the church are good at support in death but poor at support in grief. We visit and bring in casseroles. We send sympathy cards. We take off from work and go to the funeral. Then, we fall back into our routines and forget the continuing struggles of the survivors. We act as though the grief process ends at the funeral. However, we can and should help re-people the empty space. For example, when a deacon died leaving a twelve-year-old son, another man in the church who also had a twelve-year-old son took both of the boys fishing regularly.

Second, we try to spare the survivors by not mentioning

the deceased. As one widow wondered, "How could all of my friends have forgotten Jim so completely? They don't even mention his name any more!" We can encourage the grief process by bringing up the deceased's name in conversation and allowing ventilation of feelings.

The readjustment phase is the time for Christian growth and witness. Grief allows for testing and updating your faith. As we readjust, we can reaffirm our faith. After all, when we know Christ, we can grieve with hope (1 Thess. 4:13). Even the funeral service can be an experience of praise of God's support.

What's the Purpose of a Funeral?

A funeral is both a family ceremony and a community event. First, a funeral shows the strength of our "credit network." Family and friends lend us an extra measure of temporary support during the crisis of death. Their demonstration of solidarity with us confers strength. Second, funerals are official farewells. The tangibility of a body, a service, and a gathering of participants marks an important passage in our lives. Third, spiritual values are shared at funerals. Our hope in Christ is a powerful witness. Edwin Schneidman, well-known thanatologist (student of death and its phenomena), speaks of "rutters," the ancient guidebooks of navigation. These rutters described the sea lanes between where the explorers were and where they wanted to go. Our faith provides a rutter to set the tone of the funeral and burial services.

Seeing Life's Small Griefs

Not all grief involves death. Any broken relationship with a loved person or object triggers grief. Note the list of small griefs below. They are common losses but not often recognized as legitimate griefs.

- When a child begins or graduates from school or college;
- When a child leaves home for school or the military;
- When a child gets married;
- When you move or get transferred;
- When you or someone you care about gets divorced;
- When you get a promotion, a new boss, or retire;
- When you lose your health or have a limb or breast removed;
- When you go broke or take bankruptcy;
- When you lose a longtime pet;
- When fire or storm destroys your property.

The list of common losses is almost endless. Treat them like griefs, and you and your friends will respond better to these losses.

Grief—Obstacle or Opportunity?

Loss triggers grief. When we lose a loved person or valued object, we grieve. Grief, poorly negotiated, can be an obstacle to emotional and spiritual wholeness; but when grief's pilgrimage is traveled hopefully and openly, grief becomes an opportunity for growth.

- Grief is a sign of love and interdependence. Because we're capable of caring for and becoming related to others, grief indicates that we have risked growth. The death of a spouse is the most traumatic experience of any married person's life.
- Grief follows all loss. In many cases, loss is necessary for gain and growth. For example, job promotions—usually a clear gain—can trigger loss, because we surrender a position and possibly some work relationships in order to advance.
- Grief is a primary avenue for restoring equilibrium after loss. The ability to recover after loss is a sign of growing

maturity. On the other hand, the complete inability to recover our balance leads to madness.

● Grief takes time. Like all growth, grief takes an uneven route. Although we may feel grief is a three-steps-forward-and-two-steps-back process, it's more likely to move in spiral fashion. That is, we cope with our grief and learn from it as time helps heal our wounds. Then, unexpectedly, a birthday or anniversary or memory puts us into a tailspin, and we spiral back into the pit of grief and begin the climb all over again.

● Grief opens the door to growth. The Puritans claimed that suffering teaches. But suffering doesn't automatically teach us; it can only teach if we choose to learn from our pain. The secret to growth through grief lies in the answer to one question. The issue isn't what has happened to you. The secret? What have you done with what's happened to you? You can allow your grief to merge with understanding and openness to become your teacher.

There Is Hope

Sermon Text: 1 Thessalonians 4:13-16

"No hope." I had never heard that phrase before. When the doctor walked out of the hospital room, he was shaking his head. His first words were, "He has aplastic anemia; there is no hope." I stood there in the hallway trying to console the wife of my friend. The doctor gave him six months to live. His wife asked, "Doctor, is there any hope at all?" The doctor replied, "There is no hope." My friend lived almost two years before the cancer ate away all of his bone marrow. His eighteen months of grace gave his family some hope but not nearly as much as their faith did.

Paul wrote the Christians at Thessalonica to give them hope. Christians of the first century believed in the immediate return of their Lord. The early Christians assumed that all who accepted Christ would take part in the second coming. This hope sustained them, nurtured their courage, and refreshed their hearts during their tribulations. In the power of this hope they faced their trials in quiet faith. Hope was the morning star in their dark night. But the Lord delayed his return. They were oppressed and harried. They began to lose hope.

Nothing has the capacity to rob us of hope like death. We have all been told the Christian ought to rejoice when a loved one goes on to be with the Lord, but I found it difficult to rejoice when my eighteen-year-old brother was killed in a motorcycle accident. I found it difficult to rejoice when my forty-one-year-old mother died of a heart attack. I found it difficult to rejoice when my sixty-three-year-old father died. We weep at death, but it's not so much for the condition of the one who died. We weep at our own loss. It isn't bad to weep, but it's tragic if our sorrow steals our hope.

First, hope is a foundation of Christianity. Christianity is built on the fact of the resurrection of Jesus. The Apostle Paul said, "For if we believe that Jesus died and rose again, even so them also which sleep in Jesus will God bring with him" (v. 14). Do you believe in the resurrection of Jesus? Faith in the fact that God has the power to resurrect gives us hope. William Barclay comments on the difference that hope can make at death. He said,

> In face of death the pagan world stood in despair. They met it with grim resignation but with bleak hopelessness. Aeschylus wrote, "Once a man dies there is no resurrection." Theocritus wrote, "There is hope for those who are alive, but those who have died are without hope." Catullus wrote, "When once our brief light sets, there is one perpetual night through which we must sleep." On their tomb-stones grim epitaphs were carved. "I was not; I became; I am not; I care not."[1]

Death is difficult for anyone to endure when a loved one has been lost, but it is nothing in comparison with the tragedy it seemed before the resurrection of Christ.

The Apostle Paul reminded us in Romans 10:9 that if we believe in the resurrection of Jesus we shall be saved. There is hope in his resurrection. If we live in Christ and die in Christ, we shall be resurrected in Christ. When we come to know Jesus Christ as personal Savior there is a relationship developed which nothing can break. It is a relationship independent of time. It is a relationship which endures death. It is the very basis of our Christian faith. I like the way Edward Mote expressed it when he wrote,

> My hope is built on nothing less
> Than Jesus' blood and righteousness;
> I dare not trust the sweetest frame,
> But wholly lean on Jesus' name.
>
> When darkness seems to hide his face,
> I rest on his unchanging grace;
> In ev'ry high and stormy gale,
> My anchor holds within the veil.
>
> His oath, his covenant, his blood
> Support me in the whelming flood;
> When all around my soul gives way,
> He then is all my hope and stay.
>
> On Christ, the solid Rock, I stand;
> All other ground is sinking sand,
> All other ground is sinking sand.
> ("The Solid Rock")

In Jesus we do have hope. We have hope because we know death is not the end of life. We have hope because Jesus set an example in proving that death can be conquered. He indeed is the first fruit of all who sleep and promised another life to all who believe in him. Jesus said to Martha right after the death of Lazarus her brother, "I am the resurrection, and the life: he that believeth in me, though he were dead, yet shall he live" (John 11:25).

Second, hope gives meaning to death. Paul said, "But I would not have you to be ignorant, brethren, concerning them which are asleep, that ye sorrow not, even as others which have no hope. For if we believe that Jesus died and rose again, even so them also which sleep in Jesus will God bring with him" (1 Thess. 4:13-14). Paul makes it clear that Jesus will bring with him those who have died when he returns. This implies that we go directly to be with God when we die.

The Bible is quite clear on this matter. One day Jesus, John, and Peter retreated to a mountaintop. While there, Jesus was transfigured. Moses and Elijah appeared and talked to him. Moses and Elijah were not still in their graves. They had not passed out of existence. They were with the Father and could be revealed to Jesus.

On another occasion Jesus told a story about two men. One man was rich and selfish. The other man was poor and crippled. The crippled man lay at the doorstep and begged from the rich. The rich man dined in luxury and gave the poor man the scraps from his table. Both men died; the poor man went directly to heaven, and the other man went directly to hell. They both went immediately to their place of eternal destiny upon dying (Luke 16:19-31).

The Apostle Paul was in jail for a crime he hadn't committed. While serving his prison sentence, he wrote a letter to the church at Philippi and said, "For I am in a strait betwixt two, having a desire to depart, and to be with Christ; which is far better" (Phil. 1:23). The verb Paul used, translated "to be," is in the present tense. Paul had the concept that if he died, he would be with the Lord immediately. Jesus said to the thief on the cross, "Verily I say unto thee, To-day thou shalt be with me in paradise" (Luke 23:43). The Bible makes it clear that we go to be with the Lord when we die.

A few years ago Elizabeth Kübler-Ross made big news when

she started sharing startling news with the public. She revealed that hundreds of people who had died and been resuscitated had similar out-of-the-body experiences. She mentioned that people could see the body which they had left. They traveled through a long tunnel filled with unusual sounds. They all moved toward a light near which a religious figure stood. Raymond Moody in his book *Life After Life* and Maurice Rawlings in his book *Beyond Death's Door* made parallel claims.

Many years before I was aware of these findings I stood in the hospital room early one morning during the final minutes of a young man's life. He had been traveling through our small Oklahoma town at a high rate of speed, having run away from home. The police in our town began to chase him. A few miles out of town his car left the road at a bridge and dived into a creek. The police did not know he had left the road and lost him. Hours later someone heard his screams for help and rescued him. I was there at the hospital during the final minutes of his life. He was conscious to the very end. Just minutes before he died, he said to the nurse, "Nurse, would you close the blinds? The light is so very bright." It was still dark outside, but the nurse closed the blinds. He repeated again, "Nurse, would you close the blinds; the light is so bright." The nurse then turned off the overhead light, leaving the room lighted only by a lamp. He repeated, "Nurse, please close the blinds; the light is so bright." Then he died. It wasn't the light of the sun that was shining in his eyes; it was the light of the Son.

Christians cannot be separated from the love which resurrected Jesus from the dead. The apostle Paul made this clear when he asked, "Who shall separate us from the love of Christ? shall tribulation, or distress, or persecution, or famine, or nakedness, or peril, or sword? . . . Nay, in all these things we are more than conquerors through him that loved us. For I am persuaded, that neither death, nor life, nor angels, nor principalities, nor powers, nor things present, nor things to come,

Nor height, nor depth, nor any other creature, shall be able to separate us from the love of God, which is in Christ Jesus our Lord" (Rom. 8:35,37-39). Death is not an experience of separation from the love of Christ; death draws us close to Christ.

Have we permitted the despair of secular society to change the meaning of the word *death*? Death is not a grim reaper that ends this life as a harvester ends the life of a wheat crop. Death is more like the traveler who leaves one country and enters another. Death is more nearly like birth. There is a struggle at birth as a baby wants to enter a new life but is hesitant to leave the security of a mother's womb. Likewise, we want to experience life with God but hesitate to leave this familiar life. If a baby knew the love awaiting him, he would welcome birth. If we knew the love of the Father waiting for us, we would not so much fear the passage from this world to the Father's house.

Third, hope is the Bible's promise. Paul said, "For the Lord himself shall descend from heaven with a shout, with the voice of the archangel, and with the trump of God: and the dead in Christ shall rise first: Then we which are alive and remain shall be caught up together with them in the clouds, to meet the Lord in the air: and so shall we ever be with the Lord" (1 Thess. 4:16-17). Paul says there will be a great reunion when Jesus returns. He will bring all those who have died with him. We have hope because we are going to be reunited with our loved ones. The apostle was simply repeating the same promise Jesus gave his disciples. The night before his crucifixion Jesus said, "Let not your heart be troubled: ye believe in God, believe also in me. In my Father's house are many mansions: if it were not so, I would have told you. I go to prepare a place for you. And if I go and prepare a place for you, I will come again, and receive you unto myself; that where I am, there ye may be also" (John 14:1-13). We do have hope because Jesus is coming back to receive us and to take us to that great family reunion with those who have preceded us in death.

Edward Mote did say it well. The last stanza of the hymn I quoted earlier says,

When he shall come with trumpet sound,
Oh, may I then in him be found;
Dressed in his righteousness alone,
Faultless to stand before the throne.

On Christ, the solid Rock, I stand;
All other ground is sinking sand,
All other ground is sinking sand.

In the summer of 1950, we had the last reunion for the Easleys, my mother's family. We met at Lake Texhoma in southern Oklahoma. I had fifty-one cousins present for that great reunion. That event stands out so vividly in my childhood because of the tremendous fun we had. Few things in life can be more enjoyable than a family reunion. When Jesus comes back, we are going to have a family reunion. And all those who are a part of the family of faith will be there.

In the summer of 1967 my uncle Frank Easley died. He was my mother's oldest brother. She had preceded him in death by fifteen years. One of his brothers and a sister were in the room with him when he died. They told me that he carried on a constant conversation with my mother for ten or fifteen minutes before he died. They said it was like listening to one end of a telephone conversation. There was no doubt to whom he was talking. His reunion with his sister began early.

When we who believe in Jesus die, we will join a faith family reunion. Let the hope of that event sustain you.

A few years ago the psychology department of Duke University carried on an interesting experiment. They wanted to see how long rats could swim. In one container they placed a rat for whom there was no possibility of escape. He swam a few moments and then ducked his head to drown. In the other container they made the hope of escape possible for that rat. The rat swam for several hours before finally drowning. The conclusion of the experiment was just the opposite of our common conclusion. We usually say, "As long as there is life, there is hope." The Duke experiment proved, "As long as there is hope, there is life." For us who are in Christ, there is both life and hope.

Note

1. William Barclay, *The Letters to the Philippians, Colossians, and Thessalonians* (Philadelphia: The Westminster Press, 1959), p. 235.

7

I-Wish-I-Was-Dead

In the Bible Samson did it. So did King Saul and Judas. Napoleon tried it. George Washington thought about it during the long nights at Valley Forge. By this time next year, about thirty thousand Americans will have done it. What is *it*? Suicide.

Experts calculate that one-third of all suicide attempts are cries for help; one-third express indecision about whether to live or die; and one-third are deliberate efforts to die.

A Tulsa newspaper man in his mid-fifties jumped from the top ledge of a dam into the nighttime waters thirty feet below. The circumstances of his life had left him feeling degraded, a failure, fearful, and frustrated. So he jumped.

The impact of hitting the water jarred him back toward reality. Automatically he began to swim. His realization? "Instantly I knew I was a live-er—not a die-er." With help, he escaped the lake waters. Then he discovered a support network beyond his imaginings. His family rallied around and loved him. Friends came to comfort and encourage him. A wealthy acquaintance demanded the best possible medical care and offered to pay all expenses. His physician reassured him with "You were suicidal, but you aren't now suicidal." This newspaperman's attitude changed in a flash from "I wish I was dead" to "I want to live."

Phenomenon and Faith

Although frowned on by most societies and religions, suicide is a phenomenon as old as history itself. Consider these threatening statistics. Worldwide, a third of a million suicides are reported yearly. Here in America the annual suicide rate has moved above the twelve per one hundred thousand population level. Suicide is the tenth most frequent cause of death in the United States. Although it accounts for only 1 percent of all yearly deaths in this country, suicide has become the second leading cause of mortality among American teenagers. Women are three times as apt to attempt suicide as men.

But even the official suicide statistics are a bit misleading. It's believed that there are two or three actual suicides for every death recorded as such. For example, many one-car fatalities are suspected suicides. For every actual suicide, there are eight attempted suicides.

Teachings about suicide vary. Islam condemns suicide but allows martyrdom. Buddism, Shinto, and Hinduism sanction suicide under prescribed circumstances. For instance, in Japan some warriors and kamikazes choose self-sacrifice before dishonor. In *The Myth of Sisyphus* Camus, the existentialist, described suicide as the only real philosophical question.

Christianity has largely viewed suicide as an unacceptable personal choice. The Bible itself has little to say about suicide beyond the general injunction, "Thou shalt not kill" (Exodus 20:13). Thomas Aquinas saw suicide as a sin. He claimed taking life is God's right, not man's prerogative. Viewing suicide as a mortal sin led some Western cultures to deny burial in church cemeteries for suicides, to confiscate their property, drag their bodies through the streets, and even drive stakes through their lifeless hearts.

An encouraging trend is currently emerging. Whatever the religious views regarding suicide, more help is available for suicidal persons. More support and understanding is now offered to the families of suicides.

Fact from Fiction

Suicide, still generally seen as a taboo subject, is surrounded by false impressions. Actually more myths than facts exist about the issue. Consider these factual updates from the research of Edwin Schneidman, an expert on suicide.

Fiction: If a person talks about suicide, he won't kill himself. Fact: Eight of ten suicides have spoken directly about their destructive intentions.

Fiction: There's no warning for suicide. Fact: Many clues and warnings precede suicidal acts.

Fiction: Suicidal persons intend to die. Fact: Most suicidal persons are undecided about living or dying. They often gamble with death and leave rescue to others.

Fiction: Anybody who has ever been suicidal will always be suicidal. Fact: Persons are generally suicidal in short-term episodes.

Fiction: When suicidal persons pass a suicidal episode, the risk is over. Fact: Most suicides occur within a three-month period after "improvement" has begun.

Fiction: Suicide happens mostly to either the rich or the poor. Fact: Suicide is a "democratic" event, proportionately representing all levels of society.

Fiction: Suicide "runs in the family." Fact: Suicide isn't inherited; it's an individual issue.

Fiction: All suicides are mentally ill. Fact: While all suicides are extremely unhappy, they aren't necessarily psychotic or mentally ill.

Encouragement for the Despairing

How can you minister to a despairing person? Thankfully, an increasing range of resources is becoming available.

● Suicide prevention centers are usually available. When you and I are called on for help beyond our capacities, a referral is a wise option. Over three hundred suicide prevention centers are now in operation throughout the United States. Additionally, there are many emergency hot lines, crisis clinics, and counselors.

So much concern has been expressed for the rising suicide rate that a new science, suicidology, has emerged. Any public library and most church libraries contain several helpful resources on depression, support networks, and suicide.

• Be alert for a jarring loss or an accumulation of losses in the lives of your friends. Loss—of a job, of a loved one through death, of a sense of control over our lives—can plant the seeds of hopelessness. Christian faith stresses hope and believes in a secure, though not untroubled, future.

• Structure and monitoring are important to suicidal persons. Daily reassurance in the form of telephone calls, notes, and handshakes are tangible reminders to despairing persons that loving friends give form and meaning to our lives.

• Learn the high risk social signs of potential suicide. As you consider how you can help persons in anguish, be aware of several patterns of information. Certain occupations call on persons to be sensitive, idealistic, and work amid difficult conditions. Those who work in these occupations—like police officers, psychiatrists, dentists, and lawyers—are more prone to suicide than the general population. So are single adults, childless persons, and divorced men. The suicide rate among teens has increased by 300 percent during the last twenty years.

Some seasons and special times seem to stimulate a disproportionate number of suicides. The holiday season during late fall and early winter as well as the spring apparently remind despairing persons of their loneliness and feelings of lifelessness. Mondays are the occasion for many suicides. Since many of us draw our identities from our jobs, an economic downturn with high unemployment is also a time when the suicide rate increases. Surprisingly, war times are ordinarily times of lower suicide rates.

• Take note also of personal behaviors which may be clues to suicide potential: weight loss; disturbance of sleep patterns, such as awakening in the wee hours of the morning with the inability to go back to sleep; feelings of life not being worth the effort. These behaviors, taken as a composite, can be ominous.

• Don't be afraid to ask the key question: "How do you

plan to kill yourself?" One helpful test of lethality is to ask a suicidal person directly about his method of death. If a method has been chosen, it's serious. If the chosen method is in hand, it's an emergency.

We often shy away from directness in working with potential suicides. We fear we'll put ideas in their heads. If we really plan to be helpful, we'd better ask what ideas are already in their heads.

• Nothing is more important than a sense of community. Religious folks are less apt to commit suicide than people who don't belong to a church. The reason isn't theology. The difference is a community of love.

Not only is the church a deterrent to suicide, it also helps the families of persons who commit suicide. To illustrate: When a young man committed suicide, his Sunday School class supplied needed support for his wife and daughter. One Sunday School teacher opened her home to the survivors. Another church member identified the body. Money for emergency expenses poured in. Another member told of a recent conversation with the deceased during which the young man spoke of his love for his family and for Christ. This report strengthened the widow. Interestingly, the Sunday School class lesson for the previous Sunday had been on a key truth: We Christians "do not grieve as those who have no hope."

Taking Suicide Out of the Closet

Sermon Texts: 1 Samuel 28:15-20; 30:1-4; and Matthew 27:3-5

In seventeenth century England a suicide was regarded with as much fear and superstition as a person suspected of being a vampire or witch. When someone committed suicide, his body was dragged through the streets beyond the town limits and buried at the crossroads. A stake was driven through his heart, and a stone was placed over his face to keep the spirit from later rising and haunting the living. Are we more enlightened than our English ancestors? Today we also feel much the same fear, superstition, and outrage toward those in the suicidal crisis. Suicide is still a taboo, but it's time suicide came out of the closet. Let's face it honestly.

First, let's take suicide out of the closet by examining some reasons people commit suicide. In 1 Samuel 28:15-25 we see a reason why people take their own lives. Those verses record the words of a severely depressed man. In part, Saul was depressed because of his guilt. He knew he had disobeyed God. He knew he had wronged David by trying to kill that innocent man. Saul was depressed over his guilt.

When Judas came back to the chief priests and elders, he said, "I have sinned in that I have betrayed innocent blood" (Matt. 27:4). Judas committed suicide because of his own sense of guilt. He must have been tremendously depressed because he'd betrayed his best friend. People may commit suicide because of a sense of depression or a sense of guilt.

In 1 Samuel 31:4 we see another reason people commit suicide. Saul said to his armor-bearer, "Draw thy sword, and thrust me through therewith; lest these uncircumcised come and thrust me through, and abuse me." Saul was very angry— at the Philistines, at David, at himself, perhaps at God. Suicide is the most violent expression of anger possible. Most people who commit suicide experience anger, guilt, and depression.

Suicide is often a grief response to something lost. Saul had lost his kingdom. He committed suicide to express his grief at losing his kingdom, his relationship to God, and his relationship to his son Jonathan. Judas expressed his grief by committing suicide. He was grieving over his feeling that he had lost his best friend. Suicide is a grief response to someone or something you lose.

A man from Reno, Nevada, lost the finals of an "Ultimate

Urban Cowboy Contest" and became so despondent he killed himself. James Peres, twenty-four, of Sparks, Nevada, lost the casino-sponsored contest featuring mechanical bucking horse riding. Police said that after the winner of the contest was announced, Peres reportedly told a girl friend, "You don't love me anymore because I didn't win." He then went out and shot himself in the chest. Why? He was depressed over losing a contest.

The suicidal person is often one who is grieving the loss or the death of a significant person, place, or thing. Someone may lose a job, a home, an award, a relationship, a promotion, a reputation, or health and kill himself because of his loss. The suicidal person may experience guilt, abandonment, shame, hopelessness, emptiness, depression, frustration, anger, rage, or loneliness, or any combination of these. With a suicidal person, these feelings are locked in and turned inward. Such a person is often unable to express these feelings and get them out. Thus he becomes more and more depressed until he takes his own life. Suicide becomes a way to respond to the loss of something significant.

Next, let's take suicide out of the closet by recognizing symptoms. Saul gave some evidence that he was thinking about committing suicide. He began to exhibit strange behavior. He went to the witch of Endor (1 Sam. 28:7). Under normal circumstances Saul would never have gone to a witch. Rather, he would have gone to the prophet of God.

Saul continued to act strangely. He wouldn't eat (1 Sam. 28:20). Saul was a big man. It was a strange thing for him not to eat. When people are contemplating suicide, they often begin to exhibit unusual and strange behavior.

What did Judas do when he was contemplating suicide? He withdrew from his friends. Ordinarily, Judas must have been a fairly gregarious character. He had been selected treasurer of the apostles' group, but when he started thinking about suicide he withdrew from everyone.

For years Dr. C. R. Daley, Jr., has been editor of the *Western*

Recorder, the Kentucky Baptist paper. After Daley's elderly father took his own life, Dr. Daley wrote the following pain- and truth-filled words:

> The fact is his funeral was nearly four years late because in many respects he died the day mother died. He would have climbed into the grave with her any day he could have.
>
> There are some lessons to be learned in my father's death. One thing his death disproves is the somewhat prevalent belief that persons who talk about suicide are not likely to take their own lives. My daddy said it many times to many people but none of us could ever get through to him nor could we believe he really meant it.

Dr. Daley's father tried to tell people he was thinking about committing suicide, and he finally did it. Most people who are contemplating suicide try to get folks' attention.

The *Worldwide Challenge,* of July, 1980, lists several things we can do to be sensitive to the symptoms of suicide. We can be sensitive to people who have poor health. Poor health is difficult to bear, especially during a long and painful illness. People who take their own life often imagine leaving behind an image of themselves as they were, vigorous and healthy. Be alert to people who are experiencing poor health, especially the elderly.

Also be alert to the suicidal tendencies of a person who has lost a loved one. Some people have difficulty coping with severe grief. Many months after a funeral the survivor may have difficulty facing reality. He may experience panic, extended guilt, idealization of the deceased, or hostility to both family and friends. It is particularly important to be sensitive to one who has lost a loved one on the anniversary date of that loss.

Also be sensitive to people when family disturbances are present. Children are especially prone to commit suicide when their parents are having severe marital problems.

Instability in children, especially dishonesty, often leads to tendencies which later end in suicide. Children who have experienced early rejection by their fathers are prime suicidal candidates. Folks with multiple marriages or people who are alcoholics are good candidates for suicide. People with unstable occupational histories or people who have swings in their income are suicidal candidates. People with a crippling physical disability or people who are severely disappointed in the use of their own potential are suicidal prospects. We must become sensitive to people who are suicidal prospects if we are going to bring suicide out of the closet.

Finally, let's bring suicide out of the closet by intervening when people show suicidal tendencies. In 1 Samuel 28:15-19, Saul was crying out to Samuel for help. Saul didn't get any help in dealing with his problem. In Matthew 27:3-5, we find Judas didn't get any help from the chief priests. Both men were crying out for help. Their pleas for understanding were missed. If we are going to help people with suicidal tendencies, we must intervene in their lives. We must become involved with them.

I could hardly think when my phone rang at three o'clock one morning. A young woman told me she was about ready to take an overdose of drugs and end her life. I didn't know the young lady; I had never met her. Something told me she was serious about her intentions. As I listened, I could also hear depressing music playing in the background. When she poured out her life story, I understood why she was contemplating suicide. The most pressing problem she was experiencing was a husband who wouldn't support her or their son. She was grieving the mess she had made of her life. She was grieving her lost opportunity. She was grieving her bad choice of a mate. As we talked, I began to try to affirm her. I tried to reassure her that life would be good again. I kept her on the phone for over two hours until I was sure I had convinced her the will to live was better than the will to die. She promised to come by the office and see me. We made an appointment. Through several weeks of counseling she became convinced there were some reasons to live. I'm happy to say she is alive today and happily married to another man. I really believe I had something to do with her staying alive because I was willing to risk intervening in her life.

There are some things you can do to intervene in the lives of other people, but before you do you must be aware of your attitude. Guard against moralizing. Don't accuse with statements like, "You can't kill yourself; it's against God." A potential suicidal victim is already suffering from a heavy burden of guilt. Awareness of sin is one thing; but when a helper condemns a person, he may actually contribute to or deepen the individual's sense of discouragement.

If you really want to intervene in the life of persons with suicidal tendencies, then develop close friendships. Demonstrate an attitude of acceptance toward them. That can give them renewed hope. Be a good listener. We may never know how important it is just to have someone available who cares enough to listen to persons who are hurting.

Avoid pat answers. When people are hurting, they don't need to hear "Just trust in the Lord, and it will be better." Instead of telling persons about love, show them love. Be honest and sincere about admitting your own struggles. Admit you sometimes hurt and are sometimes scared.

Give such persons hope. Help them see that God loves them, and you love them. Be willing to hurt and weep with them when they are hurting, but at the same time let them see you are clinging to the hope of God's help.

Above all, don't give up on these persons. A sense of isolation is dangerous for depressed persons. If you give up on such persons, they may think everyone has given up on them. Most suicidal people desperately want to live. They just need a reason to live. If you refuse to give up on such persons, that may be the reason they find for living.

I was at East Tennessee Baptist Hospital recently when a woman jumped off the Gay Street Bridge. Everybody in the hospital was buzzing about the incident. Many thoughts crossed my mind. I wondered, *Who is this woman? Who were her friends? Who cared whether she lived or died? Why did she do it? Did she not have a reason to live?* If someone had just cared enough to listen to her, to love her, to affirm her, to support her, she might still be alive. Each of us has the will to live and the will to die. All of us are potential suicidal victims. Life's circumstances could become so unbearable that you and I might have a will to die that is stronger than our will to live. If that happened we would need someone to intervene. We'd need a friend to show us our need to live. Recommit your life to a life of service, with a promise to be sensitive to people who are hurting, and a willingness to risk intervention in the lives of people who are potential suicide victims.

8

Why Did God Let My Baby Die?

There is probably no more serious test of our faith than the death of a child. Anne Lindbergh described the kidnap death of her baby son as "hours of lead." A young mother, when told by doctors at Saint Jude Children's Research Hospital in Memphis that her son had an incurable blood disease, termed her state "a special agony." Only a parent who has experienced the leaden agonies of a child's death can really know the distress of this unique grief.

Where's the Justice?

Why do children die? No simple answer is complete enough to satisfy us. Still, the search for answers continues, with all kinds of results. For example, in *When Bad Things Happen to Good People* Rabbi Harold Kushner concludes that justice isn't always done.

I prefer the eloquent testimony I received in a friend's letter when his first child, a daughter, died two days after birth.

> A month ago at this time, my wife and I had the same type hopes for our expected baby that, I suppose, most couples have. Kathy wanted a girl. I didn't care. I just wanted the baby, when it came, to be healthy and to grow to be intelligent and playful.
>
> We got the little girl Kathy wanted. And there in the operating room, when I learned it was a girl, I couldn't have been more pleased. It continues to astonish me at how

rapidly I became attached to her. Of course, I had listened to her heartbeat before and had felt her prenatal movements, but it was when I learned that she was Mary and not Michael, and when I saw her, that I knew I loved her. She had a certain fascination for me that I had never felt before.

Most of you know by now that Mary died. She had a diaphragmatic hernia, and some abdominal organs had forced their way into the chest area thus inhibiting proper development of her lungs. She lived for slightly more than two days.

I don't really know what others have thought while they've watched their infant die. I'm not sure how they have felt, but I know I felt an overwhelming sense of impotence. God seemed to me to be powerless as well. Some might see that as a lack of faith on my part. Maybe it was. But I don't feel guilty about it. I expressed my faith as well as I could at the time, though, for the most part, I cried. I cried because my baby was dying, and she wouldn't grow to experience the things I wanted her to experience. I wanted her to see beauty and hear music. I wanted her to taste watermelon and strawberries and read good books. I even wanted her to experience human frustration and then live to see her over-come some of it. I wanted her to know life in its many varieties, shapes, and hues. But most of all, I guess, I wanted her to experience her daddy's love.

There's a lesson in that if we have ears to hear and if we realize that God is described as our daddy. Life may occasion-ally have pain and frustration in it for all of us. We may worry about what kind of world we're bringing our children into. The future may look bleak. But life, even with its frustration, is eminently worth experiencing. I wanted that for Mary. Even now, after all the pain that has ensued, I wouldn't trade my two days with Mary. And I'm sure that somewhere someone has wanted me to experience a daddy's love as well.

There are evidences in the New Testament of what might be called compensatory justice. That is, in the world to come, the poor would be rich and the rich poor. I take hope in that for Mary. This little one who had such little life deserves her fair portion somewhere, sometime. I appeal to God for that.

Where's the justice in Mary's death? With God—that's our hope and our faith.

Mourning Moms (and Dads)

There are more deaths during the first few days of life than at any later time in childhood. Almost all of those deaths occur in a hospital. What, then, are the experiences common to parents whose newborns die?

An inquiry at one medical center suggests some interesting findings. First, mourning was more intense if a previous baby had been lost, either through miscarriage or the death of another live-born. Second, feeling happy about the pregnancy made for heavier grief. Third, mothers who hadn't touched their babies grieved more. In many cases, newborns with complications are isolated or even moved to another hospital. When death occurs in these situations, the mothers feel they have been neglectful somehow. Fourth, mourning was often made more intense when the parents couldn't talk about their feelings of loss together. In some cases, the husbands felt they had to be strong for both and cut off conversations about the dead child. Fifth, the level of grief had nothing to do with how long the baby survived or the number of other living children in the family.

Mothers whose babies had died found associating with mothers of live, healthy babies extremely difficult. They often asked to be transferred to private rooms or even to a room with a mother whose child was sick. Feeding times were especially painful—sometimes made more so by nurses' insensitive offers to "bring your baby next."

Another painful concern was how to tell surviving children their new brother or sister had died.

When Kids Know What About Death

When are children able to understand the meaning of death? The answer depends, of course, on the age of the child.

By age five almost every child has observed death. A pet has died, a dead bird has been found in the yard, or an insect has been discovered in the street squashed by a passing car. How does a preschool child think of death? Most experts claim that for these youngsters death is seen as a vacation, a temporary separation. ("When's Daddy coming back home?") By six or seven, death takes on somewhat of a magical quality. ("He ate dirty food"; or "She went swimming alone after her Mommy told her not to.") From seven through eleven, death becomes more concrete. ("Grandma had cancer, and the doctors couldn't make her well.") After twelve, the adolescent is able to deal with death in more abstract, adult terms. ("Grandad's body wore out, and he died of old age.")

Because children at different ages perceive death differently, at what age is a funeral understandable to a child? Funerals can be disturbing to very young children. For instance, I went to two funerals on one day when I was a second grader. A teacher and a custodian at our elementary school had died. School was dismissed, and everyone attended the funerals. Those were the first funerals I'd ever gone to, by the way. I didn't understand exactly what was happening. I was frightened. For weeks I had trouble going to sleep at night. Now I know my reaction was typical, but then I was very upset and unsure of whether to say anything to my parents about my fears. Typically for a child, I never mentioned my feelings to anyone.

A rule of thumb to use when deciding whether or not to take small children to funerals is simple: usually don't. In general, (1) preschoolers don't understand and don't learn from the funeral experience; (2) preteens can be asked if they want to attend; and (3) teens can understand the meaning of death and the usefulness of a funeral for themselves. Since understanding a loss is necessary for grief to occur, funerals serve a purpose for some older children and for adults.

Telling a Child About Death

Death education is an emerging subject. Best done at home or at church, death education can help children understand and cope with death and grief, if certain guidelines are followed.

● Adults guiding a death education conversation should be clear on how they feel about their own deaths and the faith affirmations surrounding death.

● Children's questions about death should be listened to carefully and taken seriously. Answering the question that is actually asked is the key issue. Questions about death often trigger adult anxiety and cause us to deal with concerns that weren't even contemplated by the child.

● The most natural times to discuss death at home are when a minor tragedy, like a pet's death, occurs. These conversations should be open-ended, to encourage later questions. Teachings about Christian faith are always appropriate in these parent-child discussions. Even then, care should be taken against using religious clichés or complex theology.

One Parent's Pilgrimage

Her daughter had been killed in an accident. Trace the struggle of faith this mother describes:

> I don't think the church, in general, prepares us for Death. I'm talking about the physical as well as the spiritual. . . . I can accept Death in the old and infirm. . . . [When my daughter died] I could not help asking, "Why Lord?" Other people say they were saved miraculously by prayers. . . . I had asked several groups to keep her protected with prayer. Were these prayers unanswered? I realize no one can tell how best to accept an untimely Death, except one who has experienced it. I would like to accept the philosophy that if I expect something good to happen, it will. But right now I find it hard to do so.

This woman's struggle reached a positive conclusion, in part, because she struggled with God. After all, God understands our grief. He lost a Son too.

Facing Life's Deepest Dilemma

Sermon Text: 2 Samuel 12:18-23

Each Sunday morning John-John would come running toward me with his arms outstretched. His parents normally waited until I had finished greeting the members of the congregation before they turned John-John loose. Once I picked him up he would point to the sky and say, "Merd, Merd." That was my signal to throw him up in the air and catch him as he came down. He thought he was flying like a bird. He was one of my favorite persons in that small Oklahoma church. He had long dark hair and big brown eyes—a handsome little lad. He was named after John F. Kennedy. When he was three, he ran out from behind a parked car into the street, and his life was snuffed out by an oncoming automobile. His parents faced life's deepest dilemma when John-John was killed.

David's life shows what trauma the death of a child can cause. Nathan had warned David that his son would die because of David's adultery (v. 14). When his son died, David was guilt stricken. But David handled his grief well and developed a pattern for us to follow.

Perhaps the deepest dilemma of life comes with a death of a child, particularly a young child. The question "Why did this happen to my baby?" is almost always asked. We may not be able to answer that question, but there are some things we can say to deal with the hurt that prompts the question. Insight comes from David's experience at the death of his son, insight which will help us deal with death's dilemma. How do you live through the death of a child? What do you do when the emotional pain becomes unbearable? How do you spend the sleepless nights following the death of a child?

First, you can face life's deepest dilemma by permitting yourself to grieve. The Bible says, "Then David arose from the earth, and washed, and anointed himself" (2 Sam. 12:20). David needed to wash and anoint himself because he had been in the dirt. He had been fasting (v. 16). In the Old Testament when people fasted they often expressed self-humiliation, normally wearing sackcloth. The purpose of fasting was to excite the pity and compassion of God, whether in moments of distress or in moments of penitence. David was distressed at the death of his child and was expressing repentance for his sin of adultery.

Fasting was a common practice in the Old Testament. For example, Nehemiah heard the remnant left in Jerusalem was greatly afflicted. He heard the wall of Jerusalem had been broken down and the gates had been burned. Nehemiah wrote, "And it came to pass, when I heard these words, that I sat down and wept, and mourned certain days, and fasted, and prayed before the God of heaven" (Neh. 1:4). Fasting was a form of grief.

Jesus grieved at the death of his friend Lazarus. When Jesus arrived at the tomb of Lazarus he wept (John 11:35). The expression of grief is wholesome and healthy.

One mother interpreting the grief of Mary, the mother of Jesus, wrote.

> I heard two soldiers talking
> As they came down the hill,
> The sombre hill of Calvary,
> Bleak and black and still.
> And one said, "The night is late,
> These thieves take long to die."
> And one said, "I am sore afraid,
> And yet I know not why."
>
> I heard two women weeping
> As down the hill they came,

And one was like a broken rose,
And one was like a flame.
One said, "Men shall rue
This deed their hands have done."
And one said only through her tears,
'My son! My son! My son!'[1]

It is normal and healthy to grieve at the death of a child. Grieve when you feel like grieving. Don't suppress your grief. Suppressed grief will emerge later and be more difficult to deal with. Cry when you want to cry. Get angry if anger is what you feel. Be honest about your emotions. Face your emotions and give expression to them.

Second, you can face life's deepest dilemma by drawing closer to God. David "changed his apparel, and came in to the house of the Lord, and worshipped" (v. 20). Upon hearing news of the death of his son, David stopped fasting, changed his clothes, and worshiped. "The house of the Lord" undoubtedly refers to the tent built for the ark of the covenant in which the children of Israel worshiped. The Temple had not yet been constructed. The point is, when David's son died, David went in to worship God. He coped with his dilemma by drawing near to God.

When my wife was a teenager she had a high school friend killed in an automobile accident. Her friend was buried on a Saturday afternoon. My wife was deeply impressed the next morning to see the parents of her dead friend in church worshiping the Lord. She was surprised they were back in church so soon. But that is a normal expression for people of faith. You can best cope with life's deepest dilemma by drawing closer to God.

In another state, I diligently cultivated a family who were members of our church but did not attend. I visited them on many occasions. They would not come to church. Their son was killed in Viet Nam. A few weeks after his funeral, they started back to church. They discovered you can best face life's dilemma by drawing closer to God.

When you lose a child, you will either draw closer to God or distance yourself from him. He is the author of life and the master of death. He holds the mystery of life and death. Let your grief pull you back toward God. Establish a regular pattern of Bible study and personal prayer. Quickly become involved in the life of your church. Receive the love and support of Christian friends.

Third, you can face life's deepest dilemma by getting back to normal. The Bible says, "He then went to his own house; and when he asked, they sat food before him, and he ate" (2 Sam. 12:20, RSV). While David's son was ill he prayed, fasted, dressed in sackcloth, and sat in ashes; but when word came that his son had died, David ended his fast and started eating again. David realized life had to go on. David started eating and dressing normally again. He got back to normal as quickly as possible.

In the summer of 1952 my brother, Travis, was killed in a motorcycle accident. He was eighteen years old. My mother couldn't get back to normal. She wouldn't let my dad take his wrecked cycle away from the house. She looked at it several times a day and wept continuously. She wouldn't throw away the clothes he was killed in. Every time she saw them, her grief overcame her. She wouldn't eat, and she couldn't sleep. No one in her family had ever had heart trouble. Two months and one week after the death of my brother she died of a heart attack at age forty-one. I am convinced she died prematurely, failing to cope with life's deepest dilemma, because she wouldn't get back to normal.

Reestablish your normal routine as quickly as possible. Life must go on. Go back to work as quickly as you can be productive. Resume your involvement in civic and social clubs. Renew old hobbies. Exercise to help ward off depression. Develop closer relationships with other members of your family. Don't suppress your grief; don't evade it; deal with it; but get back to normal as quickly as possible.

Fourth, you can face life's deepest dilemma by preparing for a reunion. The Bible says, "Can I bring him back again? I shall go to him, but he will not return to me" (v. 23, RSV). Many commentators believe David is referring to Sheol, the place of the dead. The Old Testament often uses the phrase "gathered to his people" (Gen. 25:8,17; 49:29) to refer to going to Sheol; but Sheol was regarded not as a place of life but as a universal graveyard (1 Sam. 2:6; 28:15). Therefore, David seems to be looking beyond Sheol. Perhaps it was the same hope of Job in his confidence that the Lord would reign in the latter day upon the earth. Later, Christian confidence is matured by the resurrection of Jesus and his promise of eternal life.

First Thessalonians 4:13-18 promises a resurrection and a reunion in the future. The Bible promises that a person of faith dies and goes to be with the Lord. When the Lord returns, he will bring them with him. Then we who still are alive will be gathered together with him in the air for a great reunion. In John 14 Jesus himself promised he was going to prepare a place for us; where he is we will be also. He promised to return and receive us to himself. There is going to be a great reunion. We must face life's dilemma with the assurance that we can be reunited with the ones we love who are Christians.

Live your life with the full consciousness that Christians will be reunited with other Christians in heaven. I believe children who die before they are conscious of sin will go to heaven. Everyone of us who know Jesus as personal Savior will go to heaven. There will be a great reunion when Christ returns, and we must face life's deepest dilemma by holding steadfast to that assurance.

On July 8, 1973, my wife gave premature birth to a baby boy. We had high hopes and big dreams for James Kevin. He lived only two hours. I know something of the agony and pain that David experienced at the death of his son. I also know that it was healthy for me to grieve at the death of my own son. I reexamined and reaffirmed my own relationship to God; I drew closer to him. I also got reabsorbed into my work as quickly as possible. As my two friends drove me away from the cemetery that day I left knowing that my son and I would be reunited again. By God's grace we live through the dilemmas of life.

Note

1. Quoted in William Barclay, *The Letters to the Corinthians* (Edinburgh: The Saint Andrew Press, 1954), p. 165.

III

ENCOURAGEMENT FOR CHRISTIAN GROWTH

9

"I Get by with a Little Help from My Friends"

We need a tribe. So Jess Lair says. Lair claims that in order to live well in our high-pressure world we need "five shiny faces" for supportive friendship. He's right. Regularly the wear and tear of daily life creates a need for personal encouragers.

Jesus gathered a tribe, a personal support network. I must admit that for years I thought of the twelve as only a group to be taught and to spread the gospel, but the Bible has a way of surprising me and stretching my horizons. Mark's Gospel notes that Jesus called his followers together and "selected twelve of them to be his regular companions and to go out to preach and to cast out demons" (Mark 3:14-15, TLB). The twelve were Jesus' tribe of special encouragers.

Jesus needed supportive friends. Within the twelve, Jesus selected an inner circle of very special friends. Unfortunately, these three didn't consistently provide the needed support. For instance, in Gethsemane the three weren't steady in lending encouragement (Matt. 26:36-46). Peter, James, and John didn't measure up to journalist Walter Winchell's definition of friendship: "A friend is one who walks in when others walk out."

Support Points

Life has several specific moments when we need some help from our friends. Let me spotlight a few of these support points:

• When change occurs. Think of times of change when we need interpreters and encouragers: when we cope with the upsets of our teen years; when we get promoted or demoted at work; when we marry; when we begin a family; when we hit our "mid-life crisis." You get the idea. Life simply will not hold still for us. We're always adjusting to something.

Change events call for a crowd of supportive witnesses. That's because change isn't easy to handle. No wonder Peter Marshall once prayed: "Lord, when we are wrong, make us willing to change. And when we are right, make us easy to live with."

• When we fail. Failure is sure to knock us off stride. When we stop believing in ourselves, we need others to believe in us and to tell us so.

Raisin in the Sun, Lorraine Hansberry's powerful play, makes a telling point about our need for encouragement when we fail. Walter sells out to Mr. Charley and then gambles away the savings laid aside for his younger sister's education. Enraged, Walter's sister is unforgiving. Their mother appeals to the young woman to love Walter but is refused.

The mother asks for Walter to be loved just because he has failed. She asks the younger woman when persons most need to be loved. When they've done well? Or when they've gotten so low they can't believe in themselves? Then with a wisdom that is characteristic of a mother, she reminds the younger daughter, "When you starts measuring somebody, measure him right, child, measure him right. Make sure you done taken into account what hills and valleys he come through before he got to wherever he is." We especially need a caring tribe when we fall.

• When we grow. We expand spiritually, emotionally, and intellectually when friends believe in us. Their confidence makes our growth both possible and necessary.

I like what an Arab proverb observes about friendship:

> A friend is a person
> to whom you may pour out
> all the contents of your heart,
> chaff and grain together,
> knowing that the gentlest of hands
> will take and sift it,
> keep what is worth keeping,
> and with the breath of kindness
> blow the rest away.

With friends who are willing to risk holding the mirror of reality up before us, we can grow. Our tribe provides the objective, yet loving, feedback that we can use as a foundation for growth.

Balancing Our Support Needs

We know instinctively that friendships are important to our well-being, but sometimes we major on one source of encouragement and lose the resources of other support sources. Note the dimensions of support listed below, and consider how you can balance them in your own life.

● Spiritual growth provides support, but the Christian life doesn't flourish on autopilot. Either we grow in faith and works, or our Christian faith atrophies. The parable of the talents states this tough truth clearly: "For the man who uses well what he is given shall be given more, and he shall have in abundance. But from the man who is unfaithful, even what little responsibility he has shall be taken from him" (Matt. 25:29, TLB). Grow or die—that's a spiritual principle.

One time-honored method of insuring our spiritual growth is enlisting a coach, a mature Christian who can guide our religious goal setting and help evaluate our

progress. Some Christian groups have used spiritual direc-
tors for centuries.

● It's encouraging to feel good physically, or, to state the
reverse, it's hard to feel up emotionally and spiritually when
we feel down physically. Christians know well that our
physical bodies are God's temples (1 Cor. 3:16). Physical
fitness then is one dimension of our overall support needs.

● Soul mates are precious encouragers. Each of us needs a
network of friends to provide listening ears, shoulders to cry
on, and objective answers to our questions. Our friends help
us repair our lives when they get frayed around the edges.

● Supportive fellowship is found in Christ's spirit. Jesus
realized how lonely and devastated his followers would feel
after his death. Companionship, then, is one facet of his
Holy Spirit's ministry to us. For example, Jesus promised to
be with us always (Matt. 28:20) and not to leave us or-
phaned (John 14:16-18). "What a friend we have in Jesus"
asserts the old hymn, and it's a true word.

Balance is a requirement for effective support. We need
to grow spiritually. We need health. We need friends. We
need to experience Christ's companionship. We need all of
these supportive resources constantly for our own encouragement.

Declaration of Dependency

Several years ago I fell into a work pattern that left me
feeling emotionally and spiritually depleted. I needed to
recharge my batteries. I reflected on my situation and de-
clared my dependence on God and my tribe of encouragers.

We need others. New strength grows out of sharing our
burdens and bearing other people's burdens too. Dag Ham-
marskjöld claimed, "What makes loneliness an anguish is
not that I have no one to share my burden, but this: 'I have
only my own burden to bear.'" Christians depend on each
other.

Wanted—Five Friendly Faces

Sermon Text: Romans 12:14-21

If you've cried as you read *Oliver Twist* or *David Copper-field*, you doubtless wondered how Charles Dickens could write with such feeling. He wrote of life so well because he lived it so thoroughly. Beginning in poverty, Dickens' father managed to progress backward into bankruptcy, leaving the ten-year-old Charles to live in a shanty boardinghouse. His father in a debtors' prison, his mother preoccupied with pity and other children, Dickens lived alone with no advice, no encouragement, no consolation, and no support from anyone. Alone in the London of 1822, what Charles Dickens would have given for five friendly faces! He wanted them. He needed them, but they weren't there.

Romans 12:14-21 teaches us how to make friends out of our enemies. If we can learn how to make friends from our enemies, we can surely learn how to become better friends to those who are already our friends. Paul begins Romans 12 with those famous verses, "I beseech you therefore brethren, by the mercies of God, that ye present your bodies a living sacrifice, holy, acceptable unto God, which is your reasonable service. And be not conformed to this world but be ye transformed by the renewing of your mind." Paul was telling his readers to establish some Christian standards to live by. They had to be consistent in their faith and life. It is impossible to relate to a person as a friend if either of us constantly changes in our approach to life. A person must remain relatively the same for us to know what to expect of him and to guess how he is going to react to us. The same holds true for us. Paul concluded this chapter by telling us how we ought to act in offering ourselves as friends and thus become friendly.

One of the most exciting books I have read recently is *The Emerging Order.* This book says the American dream was based on the idea of unlimited natural resources. Now we realize our natural resources are not unlimited. Authors Rifkin and Howard credit this realization with the swing toward conservatism now going on in our society. They are predicting an age of scarcity. If the thesis of *The Emerging Order* is correct, there will be a much higher rate of unemployment and a lowering of our standard of living. That will add increased pressure to the family as the divorce rate will increase. When we are unemployed, when we are under the gun financially, when the family is under stress, we all need five friendly faces.

We can't wait until a crisis comes to develop deep relationships. We must develop friends now, so we will have five friendly faces when we need them. Many of us don't realize we don't have any friends until it's too late. Romans 12:14-21 gives us some suggestions on how we can be friends and develop friendships.

First, five friendly faces result from blessing instead of cursing. The Bible says, "Bless them which persecute you: bless, and curse not" (v. 14). Do those words sound strangely familiar to you? They should. In Matthew 5:44, Jesus said, "I say unto you, Love your enemies, bless them that curse you, do good to them that hate you, and pray for them which despitefully use you, and persecute you." Again, in Luke 6:28, Jesus said, "Bless them that curse you, and pray for them which despitefully use you." Somehow we get the idea God doesn't want us to pay any attention to those who dislike us. We assume he simply wants us to bless those who bless us, but also he wants us to bless those who curse us. When a Christian is hurt, insulted, and mistreated, he has the Master's example before him. From the cross Jesus prayed for those who were killing him. He asked the Father's forgiveness. There's been no greater force to move men into Christianity than just this serene gracious forgiveness which the martyrs in every age have shown.

Our first "child" was a nine-pound miniature dachshund named Zacchaeus, "Zack" for short. We gave him that name because he was such a wee little fellow when we got him as a pup. We lived next door to a doctor who had a Saint Bernard. That Saint Bernard often came to our yard and stood there towering over our little dachshund. We had a storm fence around our yard to keep our dog in. If it hadn't been for that fence, our little Zack would have torn that Saint Bernard up! Zack had the meanest bark and the toughest growl you've ever heard. When my wife Lou would get close to the fence, Zack would snap at her heels. But Lou never paid any attention to Zack. Lou knew Zack couldn't bother her. She just kept on marching right around the fence acting as though that puny, little puppy wasn't even there.

We need to pay about that much attention to the snaps and growls of these who would curse us. It's often our instinct to curse instead of bless. That response says more about us than the one whom we would curse. The natural response when pushed is to push back, but people can find that anywhere in society. People are looking for others who are big enough, gracious enough, and unthreatened enough to give some ground when pushed, to turn a cheek when slapped, and to bless when cursed. If you have that strength of character to pay no attention to the negative snappings around you, the world will beat a path to your doorstep for your friendship.

The size of a man's character can be measured by the things which make him mad. What makes you mad? What hooks you emotionally? If you are not easily hooked, then you will likely have five friendly faces when you need them; but if you snap at everyone who snaps at you, those five friendly faces will be hard to find when you are most in need.

Second, five friendly faces result from developing sympathetic understanding. Paul says, "Rejoice with them that do rejoice, and weep with them that weep" (Rom. 12:15). There are few bonds like the bond of a common sorrow. Once we have cried with someone, we form a strong kinship. Yet it's much easier to weep with those who weep than it is to rejoice with those who rejoice. It's indeed more difficult to congratulate another on his success, especially if his success involves disappointment for us, than it is to sympathize with his sorrow and his loss. Only when our own self-esteem is secure can we celebrate with those who are experiencing joy. If we do not rejoice with those who are rejoicing, it's unlikely we will be able to develop friendships with them. Love, which is the basis for all friendship, identifies with both the highs and lows of others. Genuine love is joyful when our friends are happy and sorrowful when our friends are mourning. The real friend is the one who can stand beside his fellowman and have time and room for him in real human joy and real human sorrow.

A married couple I know have more friends than just about anybody. They have sympathetic understanding. The man is a veterinarian. When they first moved to our city in another state, they borrowed $150,000 to buy their medical practice. They drove a ten-year-old car for several years after moving to our town. Yet every Thanksgiving and Christmas they would spend money lavishly buying food and giving it to the poor. When any of their friends were experiencing grief, they were always among the first to share in their grief. When any of their friends were building a new house or buying a new car, they were the first to rejoice with them. This couple has the capacity to rejoice with those who are rejoicing and weep with those who are weeping. Sympathetic understanding works in their Christian lives.

Have you ever noticed how we often apologize for the good things in life that happen to us? Why do we apologize for our blessings? Is it because we are afraid of others' inability to rejoice with us? If you want a friend, weep with your acquaintances when they are in pain and rejoice with them when good things come their way. When you are able to relate to others with a sympathetic understanding, then you will find five friendly faces when you need them.

Third, five friendly faces result from a likable humility. The Bible says, "Be of the same mind one toward another. Mind not high things, but condescend to men of low estate. Be not wise in your own conceits" (Rom. 12:16). Likable humility draws a circle of love around the unlovely and, having excluded snobbery, invites all men to full privileges of fellowship. Love seeks harmony among all Christians (2 Cor. 13:11 and Phil. 2:2). The real danger of conceit is it closes the door to genuine fellowship (Prov. 3:7). We can avoid pride and snobbishness if we remember the standards by which the world judges a man are not necessarily the standards by which God judges him. Saintliness has nothing to do with rank, wealth, prestige, or birth. There is nothing more certain to destroy mutual respect than a haughty spirit. Those who are deceived into thinking more highly of themselves than they have any right to do will cut off themselves from their fellowman. So if we are going to be friends and to make friends, we must approach life with a deep sense of humility and a willingness to include anyone in our circle of friends.

All of us are repulsed by the attitude of the man who got into a New York City taxi, and said, "Take me anywhere. I've got business all over." The next time you start to believe you are indispensable, stick your finger in a bowl of water. Then remove it and see the impression you've made.

We aren't to do away with self-esteem, but this doesn't mean living under the delusion of false pride. We are to have a healthy appreciation for ourselves as children of God, but we aren't to have an overestimation of our own importance. If you really want to have friends you may need to stop tooting your own horn, guiding all conversation toward yourself, and reminding others of your virtues and accomplishments. Instead, start showing interest in others. Ask about their concerns. Tell them how important they are to you.

Fourth, five friendly faces are the result of integrity. Integrity is rare in our society. A man said to his friend, "My grocer gave me a phony dollar bill this morning. You can't trust anyone these days." His friend responded, "Let's see it." The first man replied, "I don't have it anymore. I passed it on at the drugstore."

How foreign that attitude is to the integrity Paul talked about in verses 17-18! He said, "Recompense to no man evil for evil. Provide things honest in the sight of all men. If it be possible, as much as lieth in you, live peaceably with all men." In Matthew 5:23-24; 1 Thessalonians 5:15; 1 Peter 3:9; and 1 Corinthians 13:5-6, the Bible makes it clear that love never repays evil for evil. Love always repays evil with goodness. Verse 18 of our text says we are to live peaceably with all men. Remember that Paul adds two qualifications for this. He says, "If it be possible," we are to "live peaceably with all men." There may come a time when the claims of Christ upon our lives cause us to stand for some things that will offend others. Christianity is not an easygoing tolerance which will accept anything. A time may come when battles have to be fought, and the Christian must not shirk responsibility.

Paul also says we are to live peaceably, "as much as possible" (Rom. 12:18, TLB). Paul knew very well it is easier for some to live in peace than it is for others. He knew that one man can control as much temper in an hour as another man can in a lifetime. Remember that goodness is a great deal easier for some people than it is for others. If we remember that, it will keep us from both criticism and discouragement.

In John Steinbeck's novel *Of Mice and Men*, George and Lennie are two main characters who are friends. George is small and smart; Lennie is big and dumb. They become partners and bum around the country. They finally locate a job with a rancher. Curley, the rancher's son, is an arrogant little fellow. No one can get along with Curley. He married a tramp of a girl who found it impossible to be faithful to any one man. One night when Curley was gone, his wife came down to the barn where the Negro servant lived. The Negro was not even allowed to live in the bunkhouse with the other cowboys. When Curley's wife made advances toward Crooks, the Negro, he responded, "Maybe you . . . better go, I ain't sure I want you in here no more. A colored man got to have some rights even if he don't like em." Crooks is the real hero of the story. Here is a man who has honor and integrity.

It's impossible to make friends with people we can't trust. We will not be able to share personal information with people who can't keep confidences. Personal information and experiences are the seedbeds out of which friendships grow. If you can't find five friendly faces it may be because you can't keep a secret. Deep, long lasting friendships can only exist on the foundations of trust and intimacy. Neither are possible unless we have integrity.

Fifth, five friendly faces result from kindness. The Bible says, "Dearly beloved, avenge not yourselves, but rather give place unto wrath: for it is written, Vengeance is mine; I will repay, saith the Lord. Therefore if thine enemy hunger, feed him; if he thirst, give him drink: for in so doing thou shalt heap coals of fire on his head. Be not overcome of evil, but overcome evil with good" (Rom. 12:19-21). Many have misinterpreted this passage. Paul makes it clear in verse 19 that we are supposed to be kind, not vengeful. In verse 20 he illustrated how we can be kind. He said feeding your hungry enemy is an expression of kindness. He said that if your enemy is thirsty, you should give him something to drink as an expression of kindness. Then he added something rather odd; he says in these acts of kindness "thou shalt heap coals of fire on his head." Heaping coals of fire on anyone's head sounds like a strange way of showing kindness. What did Paul mean? First-century homemakers kept a fire going in their ovens at all times. Once a fire went out, it was very difficult to get another fire going—without today's matches. When an oven fire went out, the housewife went to a neighbor and borrowed some coals. A woman normally carried those coals in a container on top of her head. One of the kindest things you could do was to lend a neighbor some coals with which to start her own fire. Possibly Paul was saying when your neighbor needs some coals to start a fire, even if your neighbor is an enemy, you should give your neighbor the coals. Don't take vengeance but overcome evil with good.

Recently I saw the movie *Hero at Large*. It is the story of a young actor who was having difficulty finding a job. He finally lowered himself to work as a promotional man for a movie about a superman figure. He went into a store one night to buy some milk, still dressed in his costume. Two young thugs came in to rob the store. The young actor took off his overcoat, jumped out in his superman-style costume, and chased off the thugs. He did it simply to help the older couple who owned the Mom and Pop store. The older couple called a television station and reported his heroics. As the story develops, the entire city of New York became wrapped up in the excitement of having a hero who would stop crime, right wrongs, and fight for justice. Everyone loved Captain Amazing. They fell in love with him simply because he wanted to show kindness to those who were being mistreated.

How long has it been since you did something good for someone who really didn't like you? How long has it been since you did something good for someone and didn't want to take any credit for it? All of us have a time in our life when we need five friendly faces. How can we assure ourselves of having those five friendly faces when we need them? Develop them now. And the best way to develop them is to be a friend.

10

Building a Home Inside Your House

Homes teach the things that make life worthwhile:
- a conscience to guide values;
- a set of beliefs to live by;
- a cause to believe in;
- a love to cultivate;
- a dream to pursue.

Creating a sturdy, Christian home is a lifelong process. John Dexter of the Metropolitan Opera was asked the ideal amount of rehearsal time needed to prepare a piece of Bertolt Brecht's music. His answer applies to family life development too. "Always one week more," Dexter replied. A good home calls for an ongoing commitment.

How Long Does It Take?

Most of us who choose marriage and family as our life-style quickly learn one foundational truth: Our relationships change over a period of time. Rather than "a marriage" or "one family," change constantly alters our marriage and family. Even if I stay married to the same person all my life and if I have no additional children, I still experience several marriages and families as my relationships at home grow or deteriorate.

Leo Rosten observes, "No two children are ever born into the same family." I know that's true. I was born an only child. Four years later my brother was born, and I ceased being an only child but was promoted to elder brother status. After another four years, my second brother was born into a family which then numbered four. It was one family, yet always different and changing. The process reverses itself after a couple of decades, of course, when the home begins to empty. Then the family changes texture again radically.

We discover several marriages within our marriage and several families within our family over a lifetime. Like spring, summer, fall, and winter, we live through seasons of home life. Christian growth requires rededications of faith at each family stage.

The Seasons of Marriage and Family

One key to a home full of encouragement is an awareness of the unfolding quality of your marriage. There are several predictable seasons of home living. Encouragement is needed for every stage of home life.

• Your "Happily-Ever-After" Home. Newlyweds believe in eternal happiness—for a while. Then the "I never knews" set in. I never knew you'd be moody every morning. I never knew you'd call your mother every Sunday. I never knew you'd stop putting your best foot forward. Romance has been confronted by reality. The honeymoon's over, and the real relationship now has to be developed. Balanced, mature encouragement is needed when "I do" turns into "I never knew."

• Your "Making-Ends-Meet" Home. Regardless of the original plan, many homes find two paychecks are necessary for necessities. A majority of wives now work outside the home. Encouragement is welcomed by adults who try to balance home and career. A growing number of homes face dual careers as an ongoing state, not a temporary stage.

• Your "Bundle-of-Joy" Home. The birth of the first child

marks an important event in the life of a family. Modern couples are viewing childbearing in new ways. First, child-bearing is often delayed until around age thirty. Second, child care becomes a third career squeezed in between the husband-wife relationship and work responsibilities. A frequent surprise for both parents is that their "bundle of joy" can also become a rival and strain husband-wife relationships.

• Your "Expanding-World" Home. Child rearing expands your world quickly. Your child soon develops a schedule, a circle of personal friends, and launches out into the world of education. As an individual, you're putting down roots and climbing career ladders. It's a dynamic era and calls for some stable encouragers.

• Your "Breaking-Away" Home. Teens storm the parental fortress. They challenge their parents' life-styles and experiment in order to find their own values. While the children are kicking up a fuss, your marriage may fall into a routine of sameness. Taking our spouses for granted and centering on our children is easy. The tough job is to keep the husband-wife relationship vital.

• Your "Untying-the-Apron-Strings" Home. Deliberately releasing your children to adulthood and watching your family shrink can be exciting; but for many, untying the apron strings takes on the quality of a deadline. In spite of the anxiety involved, we either learn to pass the torch to the next generation or they break away from our grasp. Support is necessary for this stage of home living too.

• Your "Empty-Nest" Home. A friend of mine described the empty nest in one sentence. "This morning my wife and I had breakfast at home alone," he said, "for the first time in twenty-five years." No children left at home. Coupleness again. The strength of the basic husband-wife relationship is now apparent. Grandparenthood also is now likely. Receiving our own parents or even taking our children back into our home after job loss or divorce becomes a bittersweet experience.

● Your "Three-Generation" Home. When grandparents, parents, and children move about in the same family circle, unique problems and opportunities emerge. Grandparents can provide the continuity of family history. Adult children can be accepted as peers, and the death of your spouse creates singleness again.

Other Family Patterns

Singleness and remarriage after divorce are both increasing as family patterns for churchgoers. Neither is an easy life-style in most congregations. Singles find couples generally fit in better around the church. Formerly marrieds often feel excluded too.

One churchwoman had been married three times. Her first two husbands died. Her third husband abandoned her, and she divorced him. The difference in the church's response? No casseroles. When her first two husbands died, her church rallied to her aid with visits, cards, food, and a funeral service; but her congregation had no support for her when she became a divorcée. They didn't bring in casseroles or consolation. Bitterly she observed, "I should have killed him. The church at least knows how to forgive murder!"

Faith Updates

Life isn't static. Neither is a person's faith. A faith which sustained you as a single person may not be sufficient for marriage. Faith strong enough for a couple may need updating when children are born. Faith must grow when the demands of marriage and family change. Recommitment—periodic updating of faith—provides a solid foundation for building a Christian home in your house!

Strengthening Your Family
Sermon Text: Matthew 19:3-6

In 1965 Charles Shedd wrote *Letters to Karen*. This book was a collection of letters Shedd wrote to his daughter immediately after she married Vincent, his new son-in-law. The letters were written primarily to Karen to help her be a better wife and to strengthen her relationship to Vincent. He gave his daughter some tremendous advice, advice that would strengthen any family. Charlie Shedd explained what Karen should do and said very little about the negatives, what she shouldn't do.

During the ministry of our Lord the Pharisees came to him with a negative, tricky, deceitful question. They asked him, "Is it lawful for a man to divorce his wife for any cause?" Jesus didn't really deal with their negative question. Instead he chose to answer them by giving them some positive advice on how to strengthen the family. No nation has ever had a higher view of marriage than the Jews had. Marriage was a sacred duty. Marriage was not to be entered into carelessly or lightly.

The Jewish laws of marriage and of purity aimed very high. Ideally, divorce was hated. God had said in Malachi 2:16 (RSV), "I hate divorce." It was said the very altar wept tears when a man divorced a wife of his youth, but the ideal and the real did not go hand in hand. In reality the woman in Jewish law was little more than an object. She was the possession of her father or of her husband. Women had no legal rights at all.

Most Jewish marriages were arranged either by the parents or professional matchmakers. Jewish brides were often married to a man whom they had never seen before the engagement. The man also had the entire initiative for divorce. In reality, a man could divorce his wife for any cause at all, and she had no say about it. So the Pharisees came to Jesus with this question about divorce. Jesus said it was not so in the beginning. He showed that God's ideal was for one man and one woman to be together forever. He then went on to stress how they could strengthen family life.

America is reeling under the blows of an escalating divorce rate. Almost one out of every two marriages is afflicted with marital dissension and dissolution. Christians are no less affected by divorce than non-Christians. It is estimated that more than a half million people are living without the benefit of marriage in the United States. Homosexuality and lesbianism are becoming more and more accepted ways of living.

What can we do to reverse this trend? Some people want to make laws and shape society like it was "in the good old days." Others are saying that this havoc will run its course, and we'll get back toward a main stream approach of family. Some are saying the family is on its way out. I say we need a rediscovery of biblical insights. We need to apply those biblical principles so that marriages can be strengthened. These are not just idealistic suggestions. These are truths I have discovered in the Word of God, seen verified in my own marriage, and verified by other good marriages I have observed.

I've also seen tensions and problems develop in my own marriage and in the marriages of others when these principles have not been applied in the home. So I don't mean to imply that my marriage is perfect. I do mean to imply that our marriage is stronger now than it has ever been. I am convinced that the advice of Jesus on this occasion has contributed to the strengthening of our home. There are some principles here that, when applied to your family, will likewise strengthen your family.

First, to strengthen your family, practice the principle of leaving. A few years ago Ed Friedman, a Jewish rabbi from Washington, DC, and one of the greatest authorities on "family systems" in the United States, was conducting a workshop in our church. He made a statement I will never forget. He said, "If a bride and her mother don't separate, she and her husband will. It's as true as the law of gravity, if a bride and her mother don't separate, the bride and her husband will." That's a pretty powerful statement. It's biblically true. Jesus said, "For this cause shall a man leave his father and mother" (Matt. 19:5). What cause was he talking about? The cause of marriage.

The first principle of strengthening your marriage is to leave all former relationships. It is a basic and fundamental truth that you must leave your mother and father if you are going to create a new identity as a husband or a wife. A man must lose his primary identity as a son and take on a new identity as a husband. A wife must no longer be in the role of a dependent daughter; in marriage she must take on the identity of wife. This may sound like a subtle difference, but it has profound implications.

One of the great biblical truths about children is that they are always seen as gifts from God. Cain, Samuel, and Jesus are examples of children whose mothers praised God at their birth. The parent's responsibility was to care for the needs of the child and to nurture them in the ways of the Lord. Children were not considered as presents to be adorned and hoarded. The natural growth and development of children sets the stage for living out God's design in marriages of their own.

Many problems in marriage go back to an incomplete separation from mother and father. That separation may be fought by either the child or the parent. Sometimes we equate "leaving" with moving away. Newlyweds set up housekeeping in their own apartment or house. It is assumed they have left their parents and established their own home. But leaving is more complicated than moving a body, a bed, and a table. In a deeper sense, "leaving" means separating from one family unit in order to establish a new unit. Leaving must include rearranging the emotional bonds with parents. Leaving takes the cooperation of parents and the ones who are leaving. We are never really free to establish a new relationship as husband or wife until we have clipped that old relationship to mother and father. So the best thing you can do for your marriage is to cut the apron strings and to leave home emotionally.

On the other hand, parents have a responsibility to loosen

the apron strings from their children. We must give our children as much freedom as they can handle. I will never forget the feeling of losing control the first day our daughter started to school and got swallowed up by that big yellow bus. That was in reality one of the first steps in cutting the apron strings. I know it must be so much harder to do when you cut the apron strings at marriage, but it must be done.

It is also essential for your children that they be turned loose emotionally. The ability of each partner to separate from Mom and Dad and to establish a marriage on personal commitment will be a factor in marriage permanence. A person not free enough, or strong enough, to leave his family will not be free enough, or strong enough, to make a promised commitment to someone else on a permanent basis.

If you want to strengthen your home, then follow the principle of leaving. As a bride and groom leave home, they leave something that is precious and good, but they enter into a relationship which God has also designed as more precious and better.

Second, to strengthen your family, commit yourself to the principle of cleaving. Jesus said, "For this cause shall a man leave father and mother, and shall cleave to his wife" (v. 5). Perhaps a more current definition will help us understand the meaning of the word *cleave*. If the ancient writers had been acquainted with new adhesives, they might have said, "A man shall be super-glued to his wife." That's a strong bond and what the Bible means. It is a bond so strong that the two people take on a new relationship with one another and to the family around them. In fact, this relationship is so unique it is like a new creation. Jesus quotes the Old Testament in pointing out that God made mankind male and female (v. 4). Each person has an identity and a personality which adds to the marriage. Marriage allows each partner to fulfill God-given functions. Both husband and wife bless each other. Marriage is designed to glorify God.

Some people might think when two people are bonded in

marriage they lose their own personality or individuality. That's not what it means "to cleave." Husband and wife are bonded together in a commitment relationship, but they do not submerge or lose their own personality. Sometimes we hear couples that have been married for many years proudly announce they have never had an argument. That sounds very good, and I'm glad for them. But I wonder if somebody got mashed early in the marriage and decided not to fight. The bond that holds husband and wife together is extremely elastic, as it accommodates a wide range of emotional, intellectual, and spiritual qualities of each partner. The bond will stretch and bend. It's very flexible, but it is super-glued so that it won't break. If you want to strengthen your marriage, make a commitment to cleave no matter what. If you can't make a commitment to leave, you won't make a commitment to cleave. If you don't make a commitment to cleave, you won't leave. It is essential in marriage both to leave and to cleave.

What comes between you and your mate? One of the most subtle and innocent enemies of many marriages is children. I've known mothers who would move into the baby's room when the baby was brought home from the hospital. That can be tragic. When a parent cleaves to a child instead of the mate, that parent will not only find it difficult to cut the apron strings when the child marries but will also find almost nothing left in the relationship to the mate. Are you cleaving to your child or to your mate?

So many men cleave to their jobs instead of their mates. It is easy to cleave to a book, a television, or a hobby instead of to your mate. To whom or to what do you cleave? So many marriages could be saved when the people involved are going through all sorts of identity and personal crises if they just had the cleaving power to hang on until things change.

Third, to strengthen your family, commit yourself to the principle of blending. Jesus said, "For this cause shall a man leave father and mother, and shall cleave to his wife: and they twain shall be one flesh. Wherefore they are no more twain, but one flesh. What therefore God hath joined together, let not man put asunder" (vv. 5-6). The phrase "and they twain shall be one flesh" describes a vast dimension of husband-wife relationships. Probably the earliest description of marriage in the Bible is that of Adam "knowing" Eve, his wife. The verb *to know* is a biblical word for sexual relationship. In Genesis 4:1 the Bible says, "And Adam knew Eve his wife; and she conceived, and bare Cain, and said, I have gotten a man from the Lord." Sexual union is the seal and consummation of the marriage commitment.

The Bible teaches that sexuality and sexual union is God-given. It is good and proper. Males and females were made for each other. Perhaps the only thing that God says in his creation that is not good is for males and females to live isolated, lonely lives. God made marriage to meet the sexual needs of husband and wife. In marriage, the strong sexual urge of mankind is met and controlled. Uncontrolled sexual activity is destructive to human personality.

"To know" another person sexually is to become a part of that person. The verse which Jesus quoted says in part, "And the two shall become one flesh" (v. 5, RSV). Here is a truth beyond our comprehension. The intermingling, mixing, and joining of two separate bodies, minds, and spirits into a new unity is strange and wonderful. In this mutual relationship of giving, sharing, nurturing, each person is enriched. The new being, the new blending, is the joy of marriage. Anything which would disturb or break the sexual bond is a sin.

It is often difficult to understand how two people can become one in objectives, ambitions, direction, and commitment without losing their distinctive personalities. An amazing fact about the Amazon illustrates helpfully. Several miles west of the city of Manaus in Brazil, two tributaries of the Amazon flow into the main channel of the river. One of the tributaries brings water so clear it looks like fresh spring water, the other churns with red mud. A few miles downstream the two rivers have definitely entered the Amazon channel, but the waters are flowing side by side as though separated by an invisible wall. Following the stream for a number of miles there is only a slight merger until about two hundred miles down the river where a genuine merger occurs, but some distinctive spots remain.

Marriage is a point where two lives enter the channel of mutual goals and a chosen direction. The interaction and sharing of the miles together causes some merging of personalities, but the distinctives remain. Marriage should ideally blend what is best and maintain the uniqueness of both partners in a creative, mutual stream of love and fulfillment.

These three principles of leaving, cleaving, and blending are all expressed in verbs in the original language. Verbs express action. Leaving, cleaving, and blending are all actions. We must keep on leaving, cleaving, and blending if our families are to experience stability and become a significant part of our lives. All too many families are made up of people who simply have a living arrangement in the same house. If you have applied the principles of leaving and cleaving, you can maintain a family structure. Individual existence within the family structure is not companionship or intimacy or blending. Are you interacting with the people in your family so that they're becoming like you and you're becoming like them? Wholesome blending means you are giving the best of you to them and receiving the best of what they are into your life. Are the personalities in your family blending, or are the people of your household simply existing in an agreeable arrangement? You can exist that way, but God intends for you to experience so much more than that out of life.

11
Goal: Whole!

After conversion, then what? So you're a Christian. What now? Growth. Balance. Maturity. Service. Wholeness. Christian faith is both being and doing. Christians are whole persons taking the whole gospel to the whole world. Wholeness is the growing Christian's goal.

Jesus called on his listeners to follow, take up crosses, and put their hands to the plows. Each of those invitations requires both choice and action. Christians make a conscious commitment and undertake a life-style of loving service. The earliest Christians condensed their choice and actions into a simple confession: Jesus is Lord.

A Christian Is

The Bible is full of word snapshots of who a Christian is. *Born again. Disciple. Chosen. Royal priesthood. In Christ. Faithful.* Add your own favorite descriptions of who a Christian is.

We Christians are twice created. We were created physically. We chose to sin. Then at some point we accepted Christ as our Savior and were recreated spiritually. This creation and recreation process is no do-it-yourself project. Salvation is the result of Christ's atonement. Our sinful rebellion separates us from God, but Christ's death brought about at-one-ment.

A Christian Does

Just as plentiful in the Bible are descriptions of what a Christian does. A Christian acts as *servant, pilgrim, salt, leaven, light, steward, witness,* and a *gifted one.* That's only a few of the word snapshots picturing what Christ does through us in service.

I'm not advocating a works approach to salvation. Works aren't a condition of salvation, but works are a consequence of salvation. For every gift from God, there's a demand by God. Salvation is a gift of faith. Service is a demand on our faith.

Christian faith impacts all we believe and every way we behave. Christianity is a lifelong adventure of exploring Christlikeness. Three examples—our stewardship of time, our stewardship of resources, and our concern for others— illustrate the breadth of Christian responsibility.

The Other Six Days

Christians devote the Lord's Day to worship and refreshment, but using the anniversary of Jesus' resurrection as a renewal day is only the beginning of the Christian's use of time. God owns all our days. We're responsible to him for the other six days too.

The responsible Christian's life contains a fundamental rhythm: from work to leisure to worship. These tides of living are patterned on God's creation activity. He worked, then hallowed a rest day, and finally rested (Gen. 2:2-3). The work-leisure-worship ebb and flow are natural to a balanced life of faith.

We can let work unbalance our lives, however. Laziness makes us poor stewards of our work time. Paul discovered some of the Thessalonian Christians were so eager for Christ's return that they'd retired from their jobs. They were piously waiting to ascend to heaven and depending on others for their daily bread. Paul's advice was blunt: if you don't work, you won't eat (2 Thess. 3:10). Faith is no excuse for laziness.

On the other hand, workaholism plagues our success-oriented culture. Work addiction puts your job above all else. Vacations become uncomfortable time wasters. Even worship decays into a time to plan next week's busyness. The workaholic is lopsided. His job is his idol. Balance requires work but not work alone.

Leisure is also an important facet of the Christian's life. We need wholesome changes of pace for our own refreshment and for family wholeness. Exercise, sports, and recreation help us guard our mental and physical health and keep an overall balance in our lives.

Worship is, of course, a bedrock need of the growing Christian. Worship is vital if we are serious about Christlikeness. Paul used some military images to depict the Christian's life. For example, worship is like basic training for the soldier, but fortification isn't the soldier's goal. He trains for the battle.

Likewise, after the renewal of worship, faith quickly spotlights service. Sunday may provide basic training, but the real battles of Christianity are won or lost in the Monday through Saturday frays.

How do you use the Lord's Day? How well do you use the other six days? All our time is claimed by our Lord.

The Other 90 Percent

I've tithed every dollar I ever made. I was taught tithing from earliest childhood, but I'm not sure I've always been a good steward. I haven't always used the other 90 percent responsibly.

I confess I've lived more faithful to the Old Testament than the New Testament at times. The Old Testament required a tenth of crops or herds or income to be dedicated to God, but Jesus called us to become stewards of our entire beings. Christian stewards both tithe and use the other 90 percent responsibly.

Three guidelines help us practice balanced stewardship: use things; love persons; worship God. The key is keeping these verbs and nouns correctly matched. Otherwise, I may

use God or worship things or create other sinful combina-
tions. Several years ago I overheard a waitress say she
always prayed before work because it made her customers'
tips better. I couldn't read her motives, but I wondered
uncomfortably if she were trying to use God rather than
simply worshiping him.

Tithe? Definitely. But don't forget God is concerned
about the other 90 percent too.

The Other Side of the Tracks

Two "great" Scripture passages stretch our attempts to
witness and minister in Christ's name. The Great Commis-
sion calls us to make disciples of everyone (Matt. 28:19-20).
The great commandment instructs us to love God totally
and our neighbors as we regard ourselves (Matt. 22:36-40).
Christians are expected to show practical concern for the
whole life of others—not just soul, not just body—the
entire person. All persons.

Everybody has his own burdens and blind spots. Tragically,
we can adopt an "out of sight, out of mind philosophy" and
forget others' needs. Christians have a stake in the salvation of
persons and the health of society. Burden sharing and burden
bearing (Gal. 6:2,5) call on Christians to be bifocal. We love
ourselves and folks on the other side of the tracks for one
simple reason: Jesus Christ died for everyone (John 3:16).

So You Want to Be Whole

Sermon Text: Romans 12:1-13

In April, 1968, a group of thirty scientists, educators, econo-
mists, industrialists, and civil servants from ten countries
gathered in the Accademia Dei Lincei in Rome. They met at

the invitation of Dr. Aurelio Peccei, an Italian industrial manager, economist, and man of vision, to discuss a subject of staggering scope—the present and future predicament of man. Out of that meeting grew the Club of Rome. This international think tank produced the 1972 volume *The Limits to Growth.* As the title indicates, the book basically asserts that we are running out of natural resources. There's a limit to our economic and industrial growth. The Club of Rome's predictions for the future are not optimistic.

World growth may not look promising, but Christian growth is always possible and needed. Paul ended the Roman letter with a challenge to grow. In almost all his epistles he followed the same pattern. He ended each letter with a section on practical Christian living. He was a theologian, but he was also a pastor. He could define the faith, but he could also apply it. Romans 12 begins the practical section of the book. Paul starts by telling the Christians how they can grow and mature.

Jesus' Sermon on the Mount includes the admonition, "Be ye therefore perfect, even as your Father which is in heaven is perfect" (Matt. 5:48). A deeper look at the Greek text would help us know the word translated "perfect" means mature. So Jesus here challenged his followers to become mature, whole, complete. Throughout his ministry Jesus kept saying to people, "Go thy way: thy faith hath made thee whole" (Luke 17:19). It was the desire of our Lord that every person he came into contact with be made whole. Romans 12:1-13 gives us some good advice on how we can grow toward wholeness.

We don't want to grow in some areas. After we reach adulthood, we don't want to keep growing physically. I noticed at my twentieth high school reunion a couple of years ago that some of my classmates looked as though they had just gone through a famine. Others looked as though they had caused it!

Our whole social order has been based upon the idea that continued growth, particularly economic growth, is the desired end of all society; but we are entering a period of considering the "smaller is better" theme. There may be a limit

to the natural resources we have discovered at present. Even if
we may have reached the limits of our economic growth that
doesn't mean we've reached the limits of growth. There is still
plenty of room for us to grow mentally. We have just begun to
grow in our knowledge of medicine, computers, lasers, ther-
modynamics, and outer space. We can grow mentally and
emotionally. There is so much about man that we are just beginning to discover. The field of study of human behavior is a
relatively new science.

Most importantly, we can also grow spiritually. We can't be
whole without maturing spiritually. There is so much about
God we don't know; the area of spiritual growth is wide open
to us. Do you want to be whole? Then you must develop your
spiritual life as well as your mental and emotional life.

First, if your goal is to be whole, then you must experience
genuine conversion. Paul says, "And be not conformed to this
world: but be ye transformed by the renewing of your mind"
(Rom. 12:2). Paul is talking about a radical change. To express
this idea he used two almost untranslatable Greek words. The
word we translate "to be conformed to the world" is *schema*.
Schema means "the outward form," which varies from year to
year and day to day. A man's *schema*, his outward form, is not
the same when he is seventeen as it is when he is seventy. A
man's *schema* is not the same when he goes out to work as
when he is dressed for dinner. A man's *schema* is constantly
altering. So Paul says, "Don't try to match your life to all the
fashions of this world; don't be like a chameleon which takes
its colors from its surroundings. Don't let the world decide
what you are going to be like."

The word he used for "being transformed" is *morphe*.
Morphe means "the essential unchanging shape or element of
anything." A man does not have the same *schema* at seventeen
and seventy, but he has the same *morphe*. A man in overalls
does not have the same *schema* as a man in a tuxedo, but he
has the same *morphe*. His outward form changes, but inwardly
he is the same person.

Paul teaches that to grow as a Christian we must undergo a change not of our outward form but of our inward personality, of the very essence of our being. We have called that change conversion. Conversion takes place when a man's inner life changes direction. It may not always show in his outer life, according to the kind of life he has been living; but if a man has experienced genuine conversion, his inner life changes. His attitude toward God, toward himself, and toward his fellowman will change.

Eight or nine years ago I had a phone call from a woman who sounded as if she had been drinking. She told me her son, a teenager, was not doing well in school, was not getting along well at home, and was beginning to do some things that would eventually lead to breaking the law. She asked for my help. I went to her home and met with her son and her. She hadn't been drinking. She simply was disadvantaged. I discovered that her husband had deserted her when her two sons were quite small.

I also became acquainted with a very bright teenager who was ashamed of his mother, embarrassed about the house he lived in, and who was developing a tragic outlook on life. As I talked with Mike that afternoon I was able to lead him and his younger brother to the Lord. They were both baptized a few weeks later into our fellowship. Because of their background and conditions at home, I knew it would be extremely difficult for us to keep them active in our church. We had to work very hard at doing it but managed to do so all the time I was their pastor.

I saw a real change in Mike's attitude. He started doing better in school. He started showing more respect to his mother. His life began to turn around. I read with interest a couple of years ago that he was getting married in the church. It made me feel good that this young man had probably married a Christian woman. I read in the church newsletter a few weeks ago that the couples' Sunday School class had given Mike and his wife a baby shower.

It reinforced everything I believe about the gospel to remember my experience with Mike. As an older teenager he was headed in the wrong direction, but he gave his life to Christ; he experienced genuine conversion. He was then married in the church. He now has a child who will hopefully be reared in the church and have a much better chance of becoming a whole human being than Mike originally did.

Mike is obviously further along the road than he would have been had he not taken that first step. The very first step toward wholeness is the very first step toward God. We are created in his image, and we can never be whole until we are like him. We will never be completely like him; therefore, we will never be completely whole. But we can become more and more like him. The first step in becoming like him is conversion.

Do you want to be whole? Take a step toward God. The first step is a recognition of sin which separates you from God. The second step is to ask him to forgive you of that sin. The third step is confessing before men that he is the Lord of your life. These three steps are steps of conversion. Jesus said to Nicodemus, "Ye must be born again" (John 3:7). We have no other choice. If we want to grow, we must experience genuine conversion.

Second, exercise your spiritual gift if your goal is wholeness. Paul says, "I beseech you therefore, brethren, by the mercies of God, that ye present your bodies a living sacrifice, holy, acceptable unto God, which is your reasonable service" (Rom. 12:1). The word translated "service" has an interesting history. Originally the word meant to work for hire or pay. It was used of the laboring man who gave his strength to a master in return for pay. It denotes not slavery but the voluntary undertaking of work. It then became a general term for service.

The word also came to mean what a person gives his whole life to. It means more than service. It means a dedication of life toward a goal. If we are to grow as Christians, we must dedicate our lives to the service of God. That doesn't mean all of us must become full-time vocational workers in the church, but it does mean we must use our gifts of service to glorify God.

Verses 3-8 makes this sense of service practical in the Christian life. Verse 3 urges us to know ourselves. We don't get very far in this world until we know what we can and can't do. An honest assessment of our own capabilities, without conceit and without false modesty, is one of the first essentials of a life of service.

Verse 3 also urges us to accept ourselves. We aren't to envy someone else's gift. We are not to complain and regret that some other gift has not been given to us. We are to accept ourselves as we are and to use the gift we have. That often means we have to accept the fact that service for some of us may mean less prominent, but still important, service.

Whatever gift we have is really a gift from God. Paul calls the gifts *charismata*. In the New Testament, a *charisma* is something given to a man by God which the man himself could not have attained or acquired. It is a personal, individual gift given to him by God.

Whatever gift a man has must be used. The motive for using our gift isn't personal prestige. The Christian's service motive is our duty and God-given privilege of making our own contributions to the kingdom of God. Romans 12 also lists the gifts of the Holy Spirit which God gives to the believers, but the point of the passage is that God gives Christians spiritual gifts. It is, then, our responsibility and our privilege to exercise our unique gifts.

Clyde Fant tells of a revival he preached at a little country church while he was a seminary student. He was staying in the pastor's home next door to the small church. As Dr. Fant was getting ready for church, he heard the church bell ringing. He hurriedly finished dressing and walked to the church, only to discover that he and the bell ringer were the only persons there. Dr. Fant realized the bell ringer was mentally retarded; but when Dr. Fant entered the room the man extended his hand and with a big smile said, "Hello, I'm Roy. I ring the bell." Roy was doing his best, and he was proud of what he was doing. Dr. Fant asked himself, "Oh God, what am I doing with what you've given me?"

What are you doing with what God has given to you? Not everyone will have the same gift. Everyone is responsible for the exercise of his gift. Within the church this requires a great deal of acceptance and understanding. We must accept our fellow church members for who they are. We cannot envy those who have gifts which seem "superior" to ours. Neither can we feel pity for those who have gifts which seem "inferior" to ours. We must have an appreciation and acceptance of each other and each other's gifts.

If you are to grow, you must let the Lord use your own special spiritual gift. It's yours. It's unique. It isn't better or worse than anyone else's gift. It's just different. Is your goal to be whole? Do you want to grow spiritually? Then you must exercise your spiritual gift! Being whole is a process, not an act. It is a lifelong journey, not a weekend trip.

Third, to be whole, we must live daily for God. A little girl visited her holier-than-thou aunt in the country one summer. Her aunt's puritanical attitude was in constant evidence. The aunt had the longest face of anyone in the country. Everytime the little niece wanted to do something, the grouchy aunt would say, "You can't do that." One day the little niece was walking down the road, very unhappy, when she came upon a long-faced mule near the fence. She walked over, patted its head, and said, "Don't feel bad, Mr. Mule. My aunt has religion too!" Our religion needs to show, but it doesn't have to be shown negatively.

Paul teaches us how our religion ought to show positively (Rom. 12:9-13). Paul says our love must be completely sincere (v. 9). That's what the word *dissimulation* means. There must be no hypocrisy, no playacting, no ulterior motive in Christian love. There is such a thing as a selfish love. This love's aim is to get far more than it gives. The Christian's love is a love which is cleansed of false self.

If we walk with the Lord daily, then we must hate evil and

cleave to that which is good (v. 9). We need to shun and avoid evil. On the other hand, we need to deliberately choose to love and have affection for good.

Paul tells us we need to treat the church as a family (v. 10). He says we must be affectionate to one another in brotherly love. We must love each other, as a family, because we are members of one family. We are brothers and sisters to each other with one Father. The Christian church is not a collection of acquaintances; it is a gathering of friends; it is the family of God.

A part of getting along in any family is to value other family members more than you do yourself. Paul tells us we are to give honor or preference to one another (v. 10). I've never seen a family unit get in trouble when everyone in the family was trying to outlove everyone else in the family. Neither will a church have difficulty when everyone in the church is trying to outlove everyone else in the church.

Paul tells us to follow God with intensity (v. 11). He notes we are not to be "slothful in business," but to be "fervent in spirit; serving the Lord." There is no room for lethargy in the Christian life. The Christian life is always a choice between life and death; the world is always a battleground between good and evil. Life is a preparation ground for eternity, so we must maintain our intensity in the desire we have to live the Christian life.

Christians can be optimists if we live and walk daily with the Lord (v. 12). Paul encourages Christians to rejoice in our hope. Just because God is God, the Christian is always certain the best is yet to be. Just because we know of the grace that is sufficient for all things, and the strength that is made perfect is weakness, we know that no task is too great for God.

When we are walking with the Lord, we will be practicing patience. Paul says we are to be "patient in tribulation." We are to meet tribulation with victorious fortitude. God is with us in every difficult circumstance, and he will see us through if we depend on him.

Paul also exhorts us to persevere in prayer (v. 12). If we are going to walk with the Lord daily, we must talk with him daily. A key to Christian wholeness is talking with the Lord every day.

Generosity is also an ingredient of growth in Christ (v. 13). Paul said we are to be "Distributing to the necessity of saints; given to hospitality." The New Testament insists it is the duty of Christians to practice hospitality.

When W. B. Oakley was secretary of evangelism for Michigan, the Michigan Baptist Convention had its offices in downtown Detroit. The employes of the Michigan Baptist Convention parked their cars and walked several blocks to the Baptist Office Building. They walked through an area of Detroit where it was common to see drunks, drug addicts, and derelicts. Dr. Oakley started for his car one evening on his way home. He approached a man with a shock of steel grey hair. As he passed by the man, the man cried out, "Mister, I'm not an addict. I'm just down on my luck and need a little help." Dr. Oakley reached into his pocket, and pulled out the biggest coin he had, and gave it to the man. He then went on home, ate a big meal, sat down in front of his fireplace, and enjoyed the evening with his wife. When they prayed that night, W. B. Oakley began to weep. He told his wife about the old man with the shock of steel grey hair and said to her, "Why didn't I bring him home, share our food, and give him a bed?" Walking with the Lord will make us more sensitive to the needs of other people. We will be generous with what we have.

Unfortunately, there is no magic formula for becoming whole. The Christian life isn't a matter of following a simplistic set of rules. It is becoming like Jesus. We must become familiar with his life. We must talk with him if we are to become like him. We must act like him if we are going to become like him. If our goal is to become whole, Christ is our only model.

Afterword

Jesus combined a "good news" message with a "good cheer" ministry. That's Christian encouragement in its broader scope.

"Be of good cheer!" Jesus often told folks to take heart. He met a paralytic and urged good cheer (Matt. 9:2). He healed a hemorrhaging woman and counseled good comfort (Matt. 9:22). He reassured the terrified disciples and pressed for good cheer (Matt. 14:27). He gave a blind beggar sight and helped him discover good comfort (Mark 10:49). He prayed for us and guaranteed good cheer (John 16:33). He appeared to a beleaguered Paul and reinforced him with good cheer (Acts 23:11).

Encourage. Through Christ you can give others boldness; put heart into; rally spirits; reassure; support.

Encouraged. In Christ we are made brave; shown boldness; given fortitude; exhibit fearlessness; develop confidence.

Be of good cheer. Jesus has overcome the world (John 16:33). So can we. That's encouragement for today's Christian!